Praise for *Open Services Innovation*

"I tore out page after page to share with my leaders. Rich in concept and deeply explained, this is how every business can rethink innovation to outgrow and outdistance its rivals. Not merely one idea, each chapter is a panoply of tools to move from the crush of commoditization to the edge of innovation. Give this book to your executives. If by the end of Chapter Three they haven't rethought their relationship with customers, inviting them to co-create what they'll gladly pay more for, then get new executives."

> —**Scott Cook,** founder and chairman, executive committee, Intuit

"Focusing on core competence often tempts managers to keep continuing what succeeded in the past. A far more important question is what capabilities are critical in the future, and Chesbrough shows how to ask and answer these issues. This is a marvelous book."

> —**Clayton Christensen**, Robert & Jane Cizik Professor of Business Administration, Harvard Business School, and author, The *Innovator's Dilemma*

"Large company, small business, product company, service business, developed country, or emerging economy—what do they all have in common? They are all part of the global, knowledge-intensive service economy. To thrive they will need to master the lessons of open service innovation. Here is their one-stop guidebook with important lessons clearly and compellingly presented."

> —**James C. Spohrer**, director, IBM University Programs World-Wide

"Citizens, consumers, and customers are fast changing, shaped by their collective experience. Firms struggle to keep up, trapped by a backward-looking definition of their business and isolated from new developments. One such change is the shift from products to services seen everywhere in developed and developing economies. *Open Services Innovation* shows how a business can redefine itself as a service organisation and tap into faster growth through shared innovation."

—**Terry Leahy**, chief executive, Tesco

"Open innovation pioneer Henry Chesbrough breaks new ground with *Open Services Innovation,* a persuasive argument for the power of co-creation in the world of services. And because all organizations are ultimately service businesses, this book is a useful guide for all managers hoping to renew or transform their organization."

—**Tom Kelley**, general manager, IDEO, and author, *The Ten Faces of Innovation* and *The Art of Innovation*

"We need to get out of the commodity trap. Whether you are managing a product or a service, your business needs to become more open and more inclusive in order to be more innovative. *Open Services Innovation* will be an invaluable guide to intrepid managers who commit to making that journey."

—**Gary Hamel**, visiting professor, London Business School; director, Management Lab; and author, *The Future of Management*

"Henry Chesbrough shows how innovating openly with a services mindset can make you a market leader. Read this book and avoid the commodity death trap—and don't attempt open innovation without it!"

—**Charlene Li**, author, *Open Leadership*, and founder, Altimeter Group

"Increasingly great products are merely a ticket to compete. With his trademark style of beautifully explained examples, Henry Chesbrough shows how open service innovation and new business models can help you escape this product commodity trap and bring you to the next level of competition."

—**Alex Osterwalder**, author, *Business Model Generation*

"Two-thirds of the world's GDP today come from the intangible services economy and, yet, most business leaders are still using the management metrics of the past. This thoughtful book clearly explains how twenty-first century leaders can innovate in a world where intangible services predominate."

—**Chip Conley**, founder, Joie de Vivre Hospitality, and author,
PEAK: How Great Companies Get Their Mojo From Maslow

"*Open Services Innovation* should be required reading for our entire health care system. Henry Chesbrough builds on his powerful insights surrounding the need to rethink innovation in our highly connected economy. His thought-provoking challenges to the services sector and his blueprint for creating ongoing innovation will serve all leaders charged with differentiating their organization."

—**Michael Howe**, former CEO, MinuteClinic, and former CEO, Arby's

The Open Innovation Community

Dear Reader,

To successfully innovate in the 21st century, companies need to open up and work with external partners to commercialize internal innovations, allowing unused internal ideas to be taken to market by others externally. Open innovation describes a new paradigm for the management of industrial innovation—and *Open Services Innovation: Rethinking Your Business to Grow and Compete in a New Era* translates this concept to the service economy.

Continuing the dialogue of this book—and my previous texts—and to put the theory of open innovation into practice, I have designed an online Open Innovation Community to serve as an informational resource for thought leaders, consultants, authors, business leaders, academics, and others who have a deep interest in open innovation. This forum is a digital community where the contribution of passionate opinions and sharing of best practices is encouraged—especially when substantiated with evidence—along with reactions and interpretations related to news headlines and events, and the latest academic research.

Given my deep immersion in open innovation theory and practice, I am passionate about asserting the critical need to continually sharpen one's skills, learn from others as well as help teach others, and stay acutely tuned in to business trends, challenges, and successes.

I hope you will not only visit the Open Innovation Community at www.openinnovation.net; I encourage you to engage and contribute to the ongoing discussions.

Sincerely,

Henry Chesbrough
Founder and Executive Director
Center for Open Innovation
Haas School of Business
University of California, Berkley

HENRY CHESBROUGH

OPEN Services INNOVATION

Rethinking Your Business to Grow and Compete in a New Era

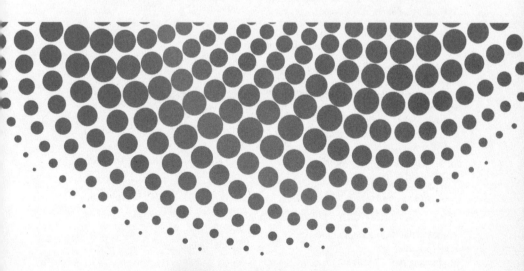

JB JOSSEY-BASS
A Wiley Imprint
www.josseybass.com

Published by Jossey-Bass
A Wiley Imprint
989 Market Street, San Francisco, CA 94103-1741—www.josseybass.com

Readers should be aware that Internet Web sites offered as citations and/or sources for further information may have changed or disappeared between the time this was written and when it is read.

Limit of Liability/Disclaimer of Warranty: While the publisher and author have used their best efforts in preparing this book, they make no representations or warranties with respect to the accuracy or completeness of the contents of this book and specifically disclaim any implied warranties of merchantability or fitness for a particular purpose. No warranty may be created or extended by sales representatives or written sales materials. The advice and strategies contained herein may not be suitable for your situation. You should consult with a professional where appropriate. Neither the publisher nor author shall be liable for any loss of profit or any other commercial damages, including but not limited to special, incidental, consequential, or other damages.

Jossey-Bass books and products are available through most bookstores. To contact Jossey-Bass directly call our Customer Care Department within the U.S. at 800-956-7739, outside the U.S. at 317-572-3986, or fax 317-572-4002.

Jossey-Bass also publishes its books in a variety of electronic formats. Some content that appears in print may not be available in electronic books.

Library of Congress Cataloging-in-Publication Data
Chesbrough, Henry William.
   Open Services Innovation: Rethinking Your Business to Grow and Compete in a New Era / Henry Chesbrough.
     p. cm
   Includes bibliographical references and index.
   ISBN 978-0-470-90574-6
   1. Customer services. 2. Technological innovations. 3. Recessions—History—21st century I. Title.
   HF5415.5.C475 2011
   658.4′063—dc22

                                                     2010043532

Printed in the United States of America
FIRST EDITION
HB Printing 10 9 8 7 6 5 4 3 2 1

For my parents, Richard and Joyce Chesbrough

CONTENTS

ACKNOWLEDGMENTS

This book is the culmination of many years of listening, learning, and reflection from a variety of people in industry, academia, and the classroom. Due to the positive reception of Open Innovation and Open Business Models, I am invited to participate in fascinating discussions. These have been wonderful opportunities to develop and test ideas and approaches to questions of innovation and, in particular, how to manage it effectively. I have come to realize that there will never be a final answer to these questions, which means that I will have a job for life—if I can keep up.

Many of the ideas in this book originated from discussions with others; some I refined and improved. I hope that this book does justice to their insights by combining them with my own and produces something of greater value. There are many people to acknowledge in the creation of this book and the research on which it is based.

I start with my colleagues at the University of California, Berkeley. Within Berkeley's Haas Business School, I have benefited from the thoughts of David Teece, Ray Miles, Robert Cole, Sara Beckman, Michael Katz, Drew Isaacs, Jerry Engel, John Danner, and David Charron. Dean Richard Lyons has been an ardent supporter as well. Many Berkeley students have provided excellent research assistance, including Alberto Diminin, Cengiz Ulusarac, David Moufarege, Kurt Koester, Lola Odusanya Masha, Margarita Constantinides, Aileen De Soto, Antoine Peiffer, Sarah Hubbard, Nadia Del Bueno, and Sohyeong Kim. Berkeley has been blessed with a rich crop of visiting scholars, some of whom contributed to this work, including Tommi Lampikoski, Mari Holopainen, Alexander Stern, Anssi Smedlund, and Jolet Van Erum. In the surrounding Berkeley academic community, I have also held useful meetings with Robert Glushko, Carol Mimura, Robert Merges, Tom Kalil, and Annalee Saxenian. Teri Melese from the University of California, San Francisco's Medical Center has also been very helpful to me.

There is an emerging group of scholars in services innovation, and it has been a pleasure to get to know some of them. Andrew Davies, Kristian Möller, Mary Jo Bitner, Rogelio Oliva, Bruce Tether, Ammon Salter, David Gann, Jonathan Sapsed, and Mari Sako have all provided comments on my earlier work that led to this book. New work in Chinese services has been called to my attention by Lei Lin; Lin and his colleague Guisheng Wu are pioneers in this field. Other academic colleagues have contributed in a more general way, including my previous coauthors, Joel West and Wim Vanhaverbeke, along with Melissa Appleyard, Ashish Arora, Jens Froeslov Christensen, Oliver Gassmann, Keld Laursen, Kwanghui Lim, Ikujiro Nonaka, Gina O'Connor, Andrea Prencipe, Francesco Sandulli, Stefan Thomke, Chris Tucci, and Max von Zedtwitz.

The Finnish Funding Agency for Innovation and Technology, Tekes, also helped support this work by supporting a conference on services innovation held at Berkeley, California, in spring 2007.

A third critical source of information for this book has come from managers of companies grappling with the promise and challenge of services innovation. I identify and quote many of these people in this book, and I won't lengthen the Acknowledgments by repeating all of those names here. Help and advice that went beyond the call of duty, however, does deserve special mention: Jeffrey Tobias of Cisco, Hyun Park of Nokia, Rhesa Jenkins of UPS, Andrew Garmin and David Tennenhouse of New Venture Partners, John Wilbanks of Science Commons, Ahmed Mohi of Fujitsu Services, Ignaas Caryn of KLM, and Daniel Fasnacht of Julius Baer. I owe a particular debt to some leaders at IBM, including Jim Spohrer, Paul Horn, Paul Maglio, Nick D'Onofrio, and Jean Paul Jacob. Despite all of their help and feedback, there are undoubtedly still many mistakes in this book. However, they are new and better mistakes than I would have made had I not talked to these people.

My friends Rich Mironov and Ken Novak have been supportive throughout this process. I am also indebted to my editor, Jesse Wiley, at Jossey-Bass/Wiley for his thoughtful comments, support, and guidance through the development and editing process.

The students in my classrooms have been a vital part of my own process of reflection on services innovation. Although they do not yet have the years of experience that my managerial sources possess, they bring a fresh perspective that challenges the conventional wisdom that often accompanies deep experience. Their questions, arguments, and conclusions have helped me test and revise my own thinking about services innovation.

My wife, Katherine, read through the entire manuscript and painstakingly exposed the gaps, errors, and incomplete thinking of earlier drafts. The book is much, much clearer for her patient reading. I am also indebted to my children, Emily and Sarah, for their support during the writing of this book. Emily in particular helped with early versions of some figures.

I dedicate this book to my parents, Richard and Joyce Chesbrough. They have been loving and supportive teachers throughout my life, a debt I can only pay forward. I dedicate this book to them as a grateful son.

INTRODUCTION

OPEN SERVICES AND INNOVATION

Some years ago, I sat in Paul Horn's office at IBM. Paul was the senior vice president of research, in charge of IBM's three thousand researchers, scientists, and engineers. We had a wonderful conversation about innovation and the many successes IBM had realized from its research activities. At the end of our time, I asked him a final question: What is your biggest problem today?

His answer intrigued and stimulated me: that his research activities were geared to support a company that made computer products: systems, servers, mainframes, and software. But most of IBM's revenues were coming from services, not from its products. "I can't sustain a significant research activity at IBM if our research is not relevant to more than half of the company's revenues going forward," he said.

This got me thinking. Innovation has always been a challenging and risky business. These days, it is getting harder and harder for many companies to compete, escaping the forces of commoditization, as manufacturing spreads around the world to lower-cost regions. With the increasing flow of knowledge and information, largely spurred by the proliferation of the Internet and enabled by technology, product life span is shortening. As new products come to market with increasing frequency and take valuable market share, more and more companies are finding it increasingly challenging to keep up and compete. Product life span is further shortened by customers' increasing demands for products and services customized or tailored to fulfill their needs better. The combination of

1

these undeniable forces, commoditization and shortening product life cycles, creates a commodity trap, an often perilous phenomenon that pulls at even the most innovative and successful companies. Innovation thus becomes a treadmill for many, and companies that do not keep up risk falling off the treadmill altogether, perhaps even dropping out of the business. In either case, these companies running to catch up cannot sustain innovation or their investments in future growth on this treadmill because it has no end and no place to rest.

Beyond individual organizations, these forces create a significant challenge to the economic prosperity of advanced economies throughout the world. As China and India rise as global economic forces themselves, as outsourcing around the world increases, and as commoditization of products continues, where will the jobs come from to provide high-wage employment for our children and grandchildren? An economy comprising companies that offer commoditized products will not prosper and will itself confront diminishing returns and prosperity for its citizens.

That's why Paul Horn's question was so intriguing. IBM's dilemma is representative of the problem that advanced economies in general are facing. Many companies and industries are beginning or trying to make a shift as our advanced economies increasingly are oriented around services. Products are becoming a smaller and smaller share of the economic pie, yet we know much less about how to innovate in services than how to develop new products and technologies. In order to grow, we have to learn to innovate in this new economic space that will define this era. We must answer Horn's question in order to sustain economic prosperity, pointed at both our businesses and the larger economy. How we can innovate in a services economy is the topic of this book and the question I will answer.

The route to prosperity in the future for advanced companies and advanced economies lies in services and rethinking business to innovate and build them. I don't mean the services involved in getting a haircut or in having one's nails manicured, although innovation can happen with them. Rather, I am referring to the knowledge-intensive services that are becoming the engine of growth for the entire developed world. Today services comprise roughly 80 percent of economic activity in the United States, and more than 60 percent of economic activity in the top forty

FIGURE I.1   Shift Toward Services in the United States Since 1800

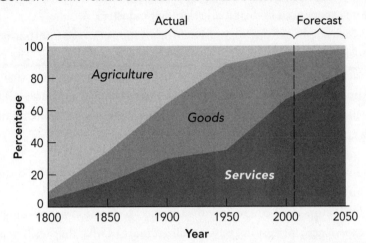

Source: J. Spoher, presentation at Haas School of Business, University of California, Berkeley, May 1, 2006.

economies around the world, according to the Organization for Economic Cooperation and Development.[1] This is up sharply from earlier times, as Figure I.1 shows. Most of this growth is emerging in the knowledge-intensive portion of the services sector, as reflected in the new jobs being created there.[2]

Innovating in services is the escape route from the commodity trap and a solution for growth, giving firms a significant competitive advantage. As they innovate into the future, companies must think beyond their products and move outside their own four walls to innovate. Do not think that service businesses are not immune from stagnation. Like commodity businesses, they too have to raise their game, but they do so in different ways, often by working effectively with products to create platforms. As we shall see, this requires a different mind-set and a different stance toward business, customers, business models, and the ability and willingness to open up the innovation process.

KEY CONCEPTS

Leveraging services innovation effectively is a challenging task that requires nothing less than a new approach to doing business. With new thinking, companies that openly innovate can reach levels of success they have never before experienced in their market or their industry.

Many of the existing approaches to innovation emerged from business models focused on product- or manufacturing-based thinking. The rise of services in this new era means that these approaches must change if companies are to be successful and sustainable. Four concepts and practices are critical to this alternative approach or way of thinking that will enable innovation and growth:

- You must think of your business as a service in order to sustain profitability and achieve new growth.
- Innovators must co-create with customers to create more meaningful experiences for customers, who will get more of what they really want.
- Open Innovation accelerates and deepens service innovation and growth by promoting specialization within the customers, suppliers, makers of complementary goods and services, and other third parties surrounding the business, resulting in more choice and variety for customers.
- Effective services innovation requires new business models that profit from internal innovation initiatives and stimulate external innovation activities that add to the value of their own business.

Together these principles create a framework for innovation that will allow businesses to grow and compete in a services era, ultimately escaping the commodity trap and that treacherous treadmill.

ESCAPING THE COMMODITY TRAP

Open Services Innovation can deliver both better products and better services for a business's customers and better economics for that business. It is the path to escape the pressures of commoditization that are hitting so many product businesses and, increasingly, services businesses too. This same path will propel advanced economies, which drive all others throughout the world, forward in this century.

This brings us back to IBM. Since that conversation I had with Paul Horn some years ago, IBM has made substantial efforts to understand innovation in services. Although many of the successes are proprietary to the company, IBM has publicized many of its accomplishments in which services innovation brought it new growth and profits. A single concept developed around business modeling has led to new services revenues in the many hundreds of millions of dollars. Another tool innovated openly has helped IBM provide quotes for its services business faster than previously imagined, helping it to close more deals, including some that it might have lost in the past. With this new approach, IBM Research analyzed its own business processes and found ways to make improvements of 10 to 50 percent in some of them, generating savings of many tens of millions of dollars. These gains are many times the amount IBM spent on the research to develop them.[3] In addition, IBM Research shares many of its discoveries with its customers through its IBM Global Services business, which now brings in more than half of IBM's total revenue.

IBM now has a services-focused business model that enables it to sustain its innovative activities in services and compete effectively, providing value for both its customers and its shareholders. The themes and framework within this book will help other companies become better able to innovate in services as well. Although the journey is long, Paul Horn (who has since retired and now works at New York University) and his IBM colleagues insist that the results are well worth the effort.

ABOUT THIS BOOK

This book is divided into two parts. Part One develops the conceptual framework and approach to Open Services Innovation. Part Two describes applications and examples of Open Services Innovation in a variety of industries, geographies, and contexts.

Chapter One sets the scene by making the case for the importance of Open Services Innovation. Chapter Two discusses the need to rethink a business from a services point of view. Chapter Three explores the benefits to businesses of inviting customers to co-create with them. Chapter Four delves more deeply into the role of open innovation in services and explains how it accelerates the path to market for firms and deepens both economies of scale and economies of scope for them. Chapter Five shows how services innovation requires a new business model in order to make effective use of these concepts.

Part Two begins in Chapter Six by describing and analyzing a number of exemplary service innovators—large and well-known companies. Chapter Seven, by contrast, considers smaller companies that are service innovators. Chapter Eight examines the ways in which services companies can develop their own innovative capability. Chapter Nine extends the examples to services innovation in two emerging economies, India and China. And Chapter Ten closes by considering the growing importance of services innovation in the world's economies and the need to enrich our understanding of how this can be measured, managed, and cultivated.

These concepts and examples set out in this book will prepare you to tackle the challenges of services innovation. Whether your business makes a product or sells a service, it must innovate to grow and compete in this new era.

CHAPTER 1

THE CASE FOR OPEN SERVICES INNOVATION

As I write this chapter, the Western world's leading economies (along with Japan's) are in a terrible state. Even before the recession began in 2008, disruptive new forces were at work transforming the global economy:

- Useful knowledge, information, and technology are now widely distributed around the world.
- Increased global competition and higher rates of growth in the developing world are leading to greater wealth and rising standards of living, while stagnation is taking hold in most developed economies.
- The advanced economics are confronting unsustainably high levels of debt that, ironically, are being financed by lending from poorer developing economies.

Let us consider each of these in turn.

The spread of useful knowledge around the globe seems like a good development at first glance. Alert companies have more places to look for useful technology, and people and companies with ideas have more outlets to which they can offer their knowledge. People who live in economies with lower costs of living can use this knowledge as well as many in more expensive areas. Therefore, the advantage of superior technology that used to be the sole province of wealthier countries has given way to a more level playing field, raising the pressure on companies in the advanced economies.

The Great Recession, as many have called it, that started in 2008 ushered in a new era among the world's economies. Most of the top economies in the Organization for Economic Cooperation and Development (OECD) suffered significant declines in economic output. Some economies, including the United States, lost more jobs than any previous economic downturn since the Great Depression. Other leading economies, including Spain, have witnessed unemployment rates of over 20 percent.

Meanwhile, Brazil, China, and India saw little loss of output from the economic upheaval. Rather, each of their economies has grown significantly during the period. Their concern now is that their economies could overheat, creating a new bubble. This growth is bringing hundreds of millions of new consumers into the global marketplace. It is also creating a similar number of companies and workers in developing regions who are increasingly able to compete for jobs in those global markets.

A great deal of wealth creation has shifted as well, away from the advanced to the developing countries. China, for example, now has 98 billionaires, and India has 58.[1] Much of the growth in the foreseeable future will have to come from the developing economies, a remarkable turn of events since World War II.

In an attempt to stave off a deeper economic downturn, many Western economies have stepped up government spending even as tax receipts declined in the downturn. As a result, sovereign debt is at uncomfortably high and unsustainable levels in many of these economies, including Greece, Japan, and Spain. For these economies, growth is at best meager, and at worst negative, which makes it politically far more painful to execute the macroeconomic policy changes needed to reverse the buildup of this debt.

Among the many consequences of these changes is one of concern over the longer term: the impact on new entrants into the workforce in advanced economies. Today young people in countries with advanced economies are finding themselves excluded from the job market as they graduate and look to start their working careers. Even those who find work often must settle for lower wages than they would have earned in the past. Moreover, research shows that many who make this trade-off will have permanently lower wages than their peers who entered the job market just a few years earlier.[2]

THE COMMODITY TRAP

These disruptive economic forces are creating a phenomenon that I call the commodity trap, which more product-focused companies are finding hard to break out of or avoid.[3] The commodity trap is made up of the following business realities:

∘ ∘ ∘

• *Manufacturing and business process knowledge and insights are widely distributed.* It is getting harder for companies to differentiate their products and sustain that differentiation over time. Products are fighting the tendency to become commoditized (commodities are products that are sold on the basis of their cost, not their value). Commoditization is largely the result of success in an industry or the product sector in general. The knowledge and insights that have been developed from work on design and manufacturing processes like Six Sigma, Total Quality Management, supply chain management, and customer relationship management have led to much higher-quality products. However, these methods and frameworks are now well understood around the world and have been encoded into software that is also widely available around the world. When the same approaches and the same tools are available to everyone, anyone can build a good product. No wonder it is getting harder to remain competitive.

• *Manufacturing of products is moving to areas of the world with very low costs.* Computers and networks are spreading product designs and process tools around the world, where products can be produced cheaply. Today Samsung, Hyundai, and LG in South Korea are challenging global leaders in automobiles, cell phones, electronics, and other product categories. These firms were far behind the leading edge in the world just a decade earlier. Even they cannot rest on their laurels, however.

Haier, Huawei, and Lenovo in China are also rising rapidly and will soon become world-leading companies. Clearly the product world is facing severe pressures to produce and sell on the basis of cost, not value.

• As challenging as the spread of best practices around the world is to product manufacturers, another force compounds their predicament: *the shrinking amount of time a product lasts in the market before a new and improved one takes its place.* As a result, even successful products can expect to enjoy an advantage in the market for a shorter time than in the past. In the hard disk drive industry where I used to work, our early products typically sold for many years. With the rise of the PC market and the incorporation of hard disks into every PC, disk drives would sell for perhaps two years. By the 1990s, even a very successful disk drive might sell for only nine months. After that, a new and even better product was available.

In pharmaceuticals, the expected lives of new drugs have also shortened. Food and Drug Administration approval now takes eight or more years for typical drugs. Then as soon as successful drugs come off patent protection after twenty years from the patent filing, generic drug companies copy them. In the largest market segments, successful patented drugs now also must share the market with rival patented drugs, even while the patents are still in effect. At least six different patented statin drugs to control cholesterol are on the market, for example.

Anyone who has purchased a cell phone in the past year can vouch for how quickly product life cycles are moving in that market. New designs and new capabilities are emerging every four to six months, which means that even very successful, differentiated products quickly lose their luster. Competing on such time intervals is like the Red Queen in *Alice in Wonderland* where one must run as fast as one can simply to stay in place. Even small missteps can cause companies to fall far behind.

o o o

Continuing to run on the treadmill isn't going to get us back to growth. We need to confront the limits of product-focused innovation and rethink how to innovate.

10

THE WAY OUT OF THIS MESS

In order to reverse these difficult economic conditions, Western economies need to grow again, and that is going to take more than changes in fiscal policy at the macroeconomic level. We must rediscover growth and innovation at the microeconomic level, within specific firms in specific industries. Macroeconomic policies help to create the conditions for growth to occur. But it is the individual firms that run the experiments, take the risks, make the investments, and harvest the results that cause innovation to occur.

In order to grow again and compete effectively, businesses must change the way they approach innovation and growth. They first have to confront, and then transcend, the commodity trap. They have to stop thinking like product manufacturers and start thinking about business from a services perspective. Both companies that make products and those that deliver services must think about their business from an open services perspective to discover new ways to generate profitable growth.

It is worth observing that services have been the growth vehicle in advanced economies for some time. In the United States, they have risen from a very small percentage of the economy a century ago to more than 80 percent of gross domestic product today.[4] Services comprise more than 60 percent of the gross domestic product of thirty-five of the top forty economies in the OECD.[5] Growth will come from services in the future for these economies. It is high time to transcend the limits of product-focused innovation and move to a way of thinking that can point the way to future growth.

THE LIMITS OF PRODUCT-FOCUSED INNOVATION FOR COMPANIES

To see the limits of product-focused innovation and the dangers of the commodity trap, let's examine a highly successful product: Motorola's Razr cell phone. When this product was introduced in fall 2004, it was the slimmest cell phone available, and its cool design made it a hot product. More than 50 million units were sold.[6] By any measure, this was a tremendous success, and Motorola was the top mobile handset manufacturer.

Three years later, however, Motorola's follow-up products and new models of the Razr failed to attract much interest. The reason was that every other handset manufacturer had learned how to make slim, elegantly designed handsets. Motorola continued to develop and market new products with new features, but these didn't seem to catch on the way the Razr had. Today Motorola is struggling in the cell phone industry and has fallen out of the top position to number seven.[7]

It might seem that Motorola was punished severely by the market because it didn't come up with another innovative product to follow up on the success of its Razr. In fact, Motorola's real failure was in its product-focused conception of innovation. Motorola thought about innovation in terms of coming up with another breakthrough product. What it didn't think hard enough about was its customers' experience with its products and what additional services it could wrap around its devices to deliver a superior customer experience.

Nokia, now the leading cell phone manufacturer and the largest handset manufacturer in the world, faces a similar challenge today. Nokia achieved enormous success in the 1990s with its GSM mobile phones. It used its superior products to conquer Europe and then aggressively moved into Asia, Africa, and Latin America. It is the largest handset manufacturer in the world today. Yet what brought Nokia this far will not carry it forward into the future.

For Motorola and for Nokia, coming up with ever better cell phone products is no longer enough. These handset manufacturers face mounting pressures from new entrants like Apple, Google, Palm (now part of HP), and Microsoft, all of them working hard to continue to innovate new handsets, either by themselves or with partners. But each is doing far more than that: they are building platforms that attract thousands of other companies to design applications and services that run on their handsets. Even if Nokia can develop a superior handset (and then continue to lead in producing superior handsets), that is no longer sufficient to provide a superior customer experience. Nokia must focus its innovation efforts on the applications and services (which support its platform) that will enrich its customers' experience with its phones. If it fails to do so, it will risk being supplanted as Motorola has been.

Nokia's approach to innovation will require radical changes.[8] This company that achieved so much with its product design in the 1990s must develop an entirely new set of innovation skills in order to create, develop, and manage a platform—an ecosystem of other companies that build their offerings on top of Nokia's.

GROWTH AND COMPETITIVE ADVANTAGE THROUGH SERVICES

Innovation in services is a clear and sustainable way to grow a business and fight off the pressures that companies are facing with the commoditization of products. By transforming products into platforms that incorporate internal and external innovations and surrounding these platforms with a variety of value-added services, companies can obtain some breathing space from relentless price and cost pressures. Although they must continue to advance their products, the real basis for competition shifts toward the entire constellation of products and services available to their customers through their product.

To see this, consider one of the Razr's challengers, the Apple iPhone. Introduced in 2007, it too captured the public's imagination. To be sure, the iPhone was a neat device. It had a sleek design, an elegant user interface, and a novel touch screen. However, the iPhone was much more than a device like the Razr was; it was a system that attracted many third-party applications and services to provide users with a wide range of experiences with a single device.[9] The iPhone became a platform. More than 100,000 individuals and companies have created "apps" that run on top of the iPhone, and more than 2 billion apps have been downloaded by customers around the world.

Unlike the Razr, the iPhone shows no sign of being overtaken by competitors anytime soon. And other recent entrants like Google, Microsoft, and Palm are also making significant efforts to recruit third-party application and services developers to support their respective innovation efforts in mobile telephony. This race will be won by those who can attract the most support and offer the best experience for customers rather than the one who can design the next cool handset device.

A similar race is on in financial services. As the Internet spreads more information to more places, many services companies now are taking on the role of aggregating this information for their users. Instead of simply creating their own mutual funds or exchange-traded funds, these companies provide up-to-the-second data on a wide variety of such products for users to consider for purchase. Others are offering commentary and analysis on these sites, providing users with a range of opinions and investment advice to guide their actions. In this way, sites such as Yahoo Finance, Mint.com, and Schwab.com are becoming platforms themselves.

Clearly platforms are important for services as well as products, a point we return to in Chapter Nine.

Companies that are making cool products must think beyond the product to turn it into a sustainable, profitable business platform. A veteran Silicon Valley venture capitalist made the point this way: "Whenever we see a business plan for a new device, we immediately ask, 'OK, where's the service associated with that device?'"[10]

THE CHALLENGE OF DIFFERING BUSINESS MODELS

Product-focused companies face another challenge in thinking beyond the product. For companies that already make products in an industry, services may represent a challenge to the traditional product-based business models employed in their industry. The role of the customer, the interaction between customer and supplier, and the design of the supply chain may have to change in a services-oriented business model. This shift toward services, which can be a saving grace from commoditization, can also engender significant conflicts within the organization. As we will see, conflicts can arise between product-based business models and services-based business models. (Apple had an advantage in this regard. It was a new entrant into cell phones, so it was not constrained by legacy business models in that industry.) We examine these conflicts in detail in Chapter Five, but an example can clarify the point.

One example of these conflicts is how to charge for services versus how to charge for a product. When selling a product, a salesperson often bundles in some service items in order to complete the sale, and usually without changing the price of the product. A product might come bundled with a warranty for a specific period of time, or free installation and training. But when a company shifts to a services-based business model, these "freebies" that were bundled in now become separate items that have their own prices. Much more sales training is needed to sell these options to customers who were accustomed to getting them for free. More fundamental, a product is usually a lump-sum purchase, while a service is typically sold as something that is consumed over time, as with a subscription or some other ongoing revenue stream. This creates a need for a different kind of sales and distribution process and also different kinds of salespeople. We will see a number of these approaches to charging for services, and some of the organizational changes they require, in Chapter Five.

SERVICES BUSINESS MODEL INNOVATIONS: THE PACKAGE SHIPMENT INDUSTRY

The discussion so far has looked at the need for products to be used as platforms to deliver a superior customer experience that entails services. But this kind of thinking is equally valuable for services businesses as well. And, perhaps ironically, incorporating some degree of "product-ness" in a services business can make the business better able to grow without creating too much complexity.

One such service innovation is the FedEx online package tracking system. This is a capability that is like a product in that every customer sees the same initial screens to generate the shipping labels for sending packages by FedEx. The customer enters information for a requested delivery into the FedEx system and receives a label (again, a kind of product) to place on the package. That same label is then scanned at various intermediate points along the destination route by FedEx. At the same time, the customer can track the progress and eventual delivery of the package through this system.

This wasn't always the case. Customers who shipped parcels via FedEx used to have to verify that the packages had reached their arrival destination by contacting the intended recipient. If those parcels did not arrive, customers understandably were concerned and needed to know where the parcel was and when it would be delivered. The online tracking system was a valuable innovation for FedEx customers. It made shipping a product much more standardized and, hence, scalable. By scalable, I mean that this process continues to perform effectively even when more transaction volume is put through this system. It doesn't break down if this volume becomes too large.

By deploying its online tracking system and making it available to its customers to query directly, FedEx responds to customers' needs rapidly, and without any human intervention on FedEx's part. For their part, the customers who enter all of the required information do not mind the time that this takes because they get up-to-the-minute accurate and authoritative information from FedEx.

Innovation has delivered real bottom-line benefits here. FedEx saves money on having to update and notify customers when packages will arrive, and customers are much more satisfied because they can obtain highly accurate information whenever they need it. The result of this innovation is higher customer satisfaction, lower costs, and better scalability. FedEx has innovated a system that can increase the volume of customer inquiries it is able to handle without breaking down and without sacrificing quality in the process. It also empowers users to take more control of the process, from entering the initial shipping information directly, to monitoring the status of the shipment whenever desired. In this sense, FedEx is letting users further into its own processes, a process we explore in Chapter Three as an example of co-creation.

OPEN SERVICES INNOVATION:
THE FRAMEWORK

We need much, much more of the FedEx kind of innovation—the open services kind of innovation—to escape the commodity trap. To understand how we can get there, four foundational concepts must be established that together create the driving framework offered in this book:

1. Think of your business (whether a product or a service) as an open services business in order to create and sustain differentiation in a commodity trap world.

2. Invite customers to co-create innovation with you in order to generate the experiences they will value and reward.

3. Use Open Innovation to accelerate and deepen services innovation, making innovation less costly, less risky, and faster. Use Open Innovation to help you turn your business into a platform for others to build on.

4. Transform your business model with Open Services Innovation, which will help you profit from your innovation activities. If you succeed in building a platform business model, you can also profit from others' innovation activities as well.

These concepts are displayed in Figure 1.1, which shows both the concepts themselves and the most important subsidiary ideas that lie beneath each one. We consider each of them briefly here. They will be developed at length in the coming chapters of the book.

Concept 1: Think of Your Business as a Services Business

Part of the commodity trap is caused by the fact that companies throughout the world have learned a great deal about how to innovate new products. This makes it harder to differentiate your product from that of someone

FIGURE 1.1 Open Services Innovation Concept Map

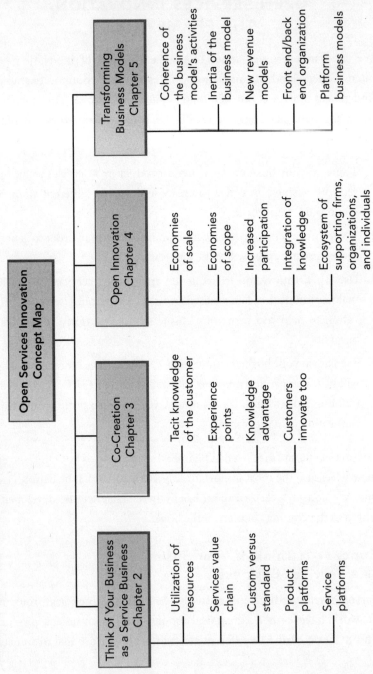

else. Therefore, in order to achieve and sustain differentiation, you will need to think about your business as a services business.

Product businesses have successfully adopted many best practices to advance their innovation capability. A few of the most important practices have now been widely adopted. Six Sigma process control methodologies help firms to manage and reduce variation in their processes. Total Quality Management instills the processes to build the product correctly the first time and to study defective products carefully to eliminate their root causes for the future. Supply chain management focuses companies on sharing information with key customers and suppliers in order to coordinate ordering and inventories throughout the supply chain. Customer relationship management helps companies reduce selling costs with their customers and develop a much better understanding of those customers at both a personal and organizational level.

Precisely because these techniques have been successfully developed and widely adopted in both advanced economies and, increasingly, the developing economies, they make it far more difficult to differentiate companies that practice these techniques from their competitors. This leads directly to commoditization, since those who invest the most in these practices and obtain the most volume will get to the lowest costs.

Customization Versus Standardization: A Tension in Services Innovation

Customers often have diverse needs. This is a critical insight, because it suggests that the future need not be ruled by whichever company gets to the absolute rock-bottom lowest costs. That customers want and will pay for variety and convenience that address their particular needs is an insight that begins to point the way out of the commoditization trap.

Think about your business, whether a product or a service, as creating a complete experience for your customers or an experience that is as complete as one you are able to envision offering. When Steve Jobs and his colleagues at Apple develop new products, they are quite clear that their vision for their new products is driven by the desire to deliver an outstanding customer experience.

A company wishing to deliver a wonderful experience with a very low-cost process thus faces an obvious tension. The ability to customize the offering for the customer to deliver the most desired outcome to him or her requires treating each service transaction individually, so that the customer gets exactly what he or she wants. Yet in order to deliver services at very low cost, the business must aggregate individual transactions together to be processed in a single homogeneous way so that the process is as efficient as possible. This is not an easy trade-off to resolve, yet a business that wants to be effective in innovating services needs to manage both customization and standardization.[11]

Your Organizational Structure for Services Innovation

Changing the way you think about your business will also require you to change the way you organize it. Traditional product organizations have structures with operational units organized along product, brand, and geographical lines. Services are usually a side organization that lack much clout and take their marching orders from the product group, the brand manager, or the country manager. These groups supplied products efficiently, but did so usually at the cost of being fairly inflexible about providing services.

Some leading companies, however, are developing new organizational structures that better manage the tensions between customized services solutions for customers and achieving economic efficiency in delivering those services. To simplify, these companies split themselves into customer-facing front-end units that are linked to standardized back-end processes. The front-end customer-facing units develop, package, and deliver customized solutions for individual clients and therefore focus on satisfying these customers. In this way, they generate revenues and profits, with the organizational clout to match. The back-end function of these new organizations provides standardized services that can easily be reconfigured at little or no cost for individual customers. The idea is for the back-end units to provide reusable elements that can be mixed and matched in different combinations by the front-end units. These back-end units thus focus on minimizing costs.[12] Figure 1.2 shows this

FIGURE 1.2 Customized Front-End Organization with Standardized Back End

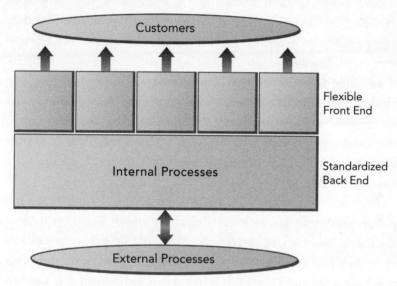

combination of a customizable front end of an organization coupled with a standardized back end.

While it is quite helpful to rethink and reorganize your business, you can and should go further by pursuing services innovation. To take services innovation to a higher level of performance and effectiveness requires inviting customers directly into the process.

Concept 2: Innovators Must Co-Create with Customers

Another aspect of advancing innovation in services is to change the role of customers in the innovation process. Instead of treating customers as passive consumers, many companies are now involving customers in the innovation process. In many cases, customers are actually co-creating new products and services.

In the world of products, companies create future products based on information received from their customers. The suppliers develop specifications to describe the product to potential customers. Once we start to think about offering experiences, though, it becomes much harder to develop specifications because much of the knowledge involved in providing, or buying, experiences is tacit. Tacit knowledge is knowledge gained from experience, and it is both difficult and expensive to write down. Learning to ride a bicycle is a classic example of the difficulty of acquiring tacit knowledge. Cooking a recipe for the first time also highlights the difference between knowing what to do and how to do it versus following the written recipe. Customers vary in their prior experiences, and suppliers vary in their prior activities as well. Tacit knowledge interferes with the ability of suppliers and customers to communicate with one another.[13]

Managing co-creation effectively requires developing ways to manage, and perhaps overcome, tacit knowledge. We already looked at the role that the package tracking tool plays for FedEx in helping customers know where their packages are at all times. Another company that has dealt with tacit knowledge quite effectively is Threadless.com, which sells custom-designed T-shirts to customers via the Web. In contrast to most other clothing makers, the company does not design the shirts. Instead, it invites anyone who wishes to submit a design for a shirt. These designs are then displayed on the Web site, where visitors can vote for the designs they prefer. Threadless tallies up the votes and then produces the top ten designs for that period. Best of all, the company has effectively presold much of its production, since the voters on the site are likely to want to own the shirt.[14]

Another example of a company that is embracing the possibilities of bringing users directly into the innovation process is the personal financial software company Intuit. As Intuit's founder Scott Cook explained in a 2008 article in the *Harvard Business Review,* Intuit has dramatically altered its approach to working with its customers. Instead of keeping customers out of the innovation process until the very end, it now builds in ways for customers to participate and contribute to their own experience and answer questions of other customers. Cook explains, "Such a [user contribution] system creates value for a business as a consequence of the value it delivers to users—personalized purchase recommendations, connections between buyers and sellers of hard-to-find items, new personal or business relationships, lower prices, membership in a community, entertainment, information of all kinds."[15]

The importance of tacit information explains why services innovators often must co-create with customers. Tacit information is hard to convey, so repeated interaction between customers and suppliers is helpful, and often necessary, to transmit it. Suppliers must work closely with customers throughout the innovation process. Customers who are involved early and deeply in the innovation process—that is, co-creation—can share tacit knowledge with their suppliers. The key is for suppliers to change their innovation processes in ways that enable customers to share this knowledge.[16]

Inviting customers into the innovation process not only helps to resolve the challenges of tacit knowledge. It also begins to open up the innovation process more generally. Open Innovation is a powerful tool to advance your innovation capabilities.

Concept 3: Open Innovation Accelerates and Deepens Services Innovation

Innovating in today's environment requires being open. Open innovation can reduce the cost of innovation, help to share the risks and rewards of innovation, and accelerate the time required to deliver innovations to the market. This is as true for services businesses as it is for product businesses. Being more open can also help turn a business into a platform for others to build on.

In an open innovation model, firms use internal and external sources of knowledge to turn new ideas into commercial products and services that can have internal and external routes to market. These routes to market depend on the firm's business model. Projects that fit a company's current business model flow through internal channels to get to market. Projects that do not fit that model need to go to market through external channels. The result is that companies get more value out of their internal R&D for both those projects that go to market internally and those that go to market externally. A company's business model also benefits from having both internal and external sources of ideas and technology to take to market.

While my earlier books have been primarily concerned with manufacturing firms that use open innovation to develop and commercialize new products, this approach can be usefully applied to services as well.[17] For example, traditional broadcasting companies like the British Broadcasting Corporation (BBC) face the challenge of successfully responding to the proliferation of digital media technologies and markets. Acknowledging that it no longer has the "R&D" capacity in-house to maintain its leading position as a supplier of content on its own, the BBC set up an open innovation community to engage with numerous external individuals and firms through a process of experiments called BBC Backstage. External developers are encouraged to use its Web site (established in 2005), which offers live news feeds, weather, and TV listings, to create innovative programming, some of which will run on BBC.[18] This greatly expands the number of choices BBC can offer to its audiences, which are economies of scope for BBC.

A related benefit from open innovation comes from the participation of many more individuals and firms in the market. With the diffusion of more knowledge to more participants in the industry, more people can experiment in parallel with possible ways of using and combining knowledge. No single person or company can hope to compete with this external explosion of potential offerings by relying exclusively on their own internal knowledge. Although such internal knowledge and resources may be deep, they are necessarily limited in scope. Experiments are organized and performed one at a time within a single entity, while they can proceed in parallel among many if that entity opens itself to the market.[19] More parallel experiments result in more variety and more choices, which foster more rapid innovation.

The best way forward for open services innovators is to become integrators of both internal and external knowledge. This enables them to create areas of differentiation arising from their internal knowledge and surround them with the many fruits of labor from an abundant landscape of external knowledge. When the internal and external elements are combined, they can provide a wealth of choices for customers while allowing the providers to specialize on their own distinctive competences. The result can be the creation of a business ecosystem in which many parties vie for the attention of the customers, who in turn benefit from more variety and more specific alternatives for them to consider.

Concept 4: Business Models Are Transformed by Services Innovation

Opening up your innovation process can greatly advance your innovation capability. But you can go still further if you open up your business model as well. Companies that are experiencing success in services innovations often have to change their business model in fundamental ways in order to sustain that success.

Business models are a way to create value for a business and then to capture at least some of that value for the organization. Once a business model becomes successful, however, it develops substantial inertia. This inertia can cause a company to miss out on new innovation opportunities should those new opportunities conflict with the logic of the business model. You can see the inertia of your current business model by looking at the metrics used to measure its success. Product-based business models focus on the financial metrics associated with products: inventory levels, gross margins, failure rates, and so on. Services business models differ in many ways from the metrics used for product business models. The key financial metrics tracked in running a services business are customer retention rates, the lifetime value of the customer, customer satisfaction levels, and so on.

Many successful services innovators have found that they need to overcome this inertia and adapt their business models in an effort to create new services offerings. UPS's business model now offers to take over the shipping department function for its customers. Under the terms of this offer, UPS becomes the shipping department for its customers and sends anything that needs to be sent to wherever it needs to be sent, and by whatever means makes the most sense. Usually that will be UPS, but sometimes UPS might send something using the U.S. Postal

Service or even FedEx—whatever is best for the company's needs for that particular shipment.

Companies that are moving to services have discovered that the shift sometimes forces them to change their business model. Johnson & Johnson, for example, now markets certain drugs, like the cancer drug Velcade, in Europe with the proviso that the country's national health service pays only if the drug proves efficacious for the patients who receive it.[20] Johnson & Johnson used to focus primarily on the prescribing physician as the key customer in its marketing. This new business model requires it to focus far more than before on the patient as the customer, tracking patient compliance and making sure that the right patients are receiving the medicine.

Organizations with services-based business models also look different from ones that are products based. In most product organizations, the services function is treated like an organizational backwater—something that must be provided, but not something that makes the difference between success in the market versus failure in the market. Moreover, the manager in charge of services rarely makes it to the senior levels of a product organization. To put it differently, product people are the leaders with the most power in product-based business models: they can be counted on to resist incursions from the services function, particularly if their own power and authority are diminished in the process.

Services-oriented business models operate completely differently. The services function, a critical element to competitive success in the market, is managed by highly capable people whose careers can readily extend to the most senior levels of the organization. Although these companies may also have powerful product people, the services executives are full partners in the organization and play an integral role in charting its future course.

If you want to assess your own organization's current business model, take a look at your senior management team and examine their backgrounds. If most of them came up through product organizations, it is a safe bet that your organization has more of a product business model mind-set than a services-oriented one. We examine services business models more closely in Chapter Five.

Combining the Four Concepts for Success

Combining these four key concepts provides the essential perspective necessary to move to open services innovation. These concepts, along with their major supporting points, are shown in the concept map in Figure 1.1, which will help you link these concepts and retain them after you have finished this book.

RUNNING YOUR OWN RACE: OVERCOMING THE COMMODITY TRAP

The treadmill of ever more similar products coming at an ever-faster pace is a race that very few can hope to win. And even the winners have to worry that someone else is readying an onslaught that could knock them off their perch in the next generation of products.

That's why it is far better to get off that treadmill and run your own race. Rethink your business as a purveyor of experiences to your customers. Invite those customers into your own innovation process, and don't stop there: open up your innovation process more generally to get the best ideas and technologies from others for your own business model, and let others use your innovations in their business models. If you follow the logic of your new approach, chances are that you will innovate your business model as well, redefining the way that you create and capture a portion of value for your business.

Your competitors will have a harder time copying your innovations. Because they are based in part on tacit knowledge, they are hard to copy. Because you have included your customers directly in your innovation, these customers will have invested their own time and self-generated content, making them less likely to abandon you at a moment's notice should another company try to lure them away. If you are able to open up your innovation process, you simultaneously increase your own sphere of possibilities and complicate any attempt for others to mimic what you're doing. And if you are creating and capturing value in new ways, competitors stuck in the product conception of their business model will be slow to understand how you are winning in the market. They will have to fight their own battles against inertia to respond to your success.

This is the way out of the commoditization trap. It requires a new way of thinking about innovation, services, and business models. The winners in this new economic environment will be those firms that develop strong internal capabilities in a few areas and leverage those capabilities by enlisting the efforts of many others in support of their business. Since the world is moving to a services economy, it is time to move innovation into the services context as well. The world is ready for Open Services Innovation.

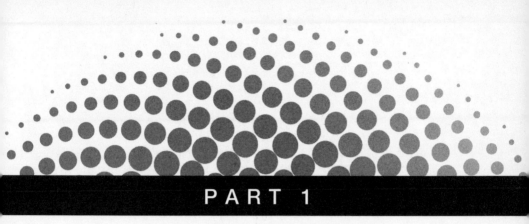

PART 1

A FRAMEWORK TO SPUR INNOVATION AND GROWTH

In this first half of the book, we explore a number of fundamental concepts that support Open Services Innovation. Chapter One has considered the impact of commoditization in products and the shortening lives of products in the market. In Part One, Chapter Two shows the need to adopt a services approach to your business, whether you make a product or a service. Chapter Three details co-creation, a new way to innovate with customers. Chapter Four shows the value of openness in services innovation. And Chapter Five explains how your business model will change as a result of Open Services Innovation. Part Two will then integrate all of the concepts explored in this part.

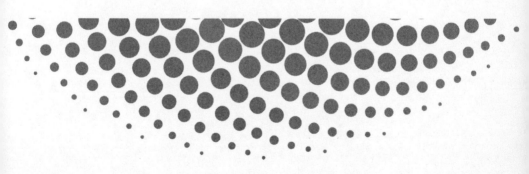

CHAPTER 2

THINK OF YOUR BUSINESS AS A SERVICES BUSINESS

The way you think about your business changes when you frame it as a service. How you relate to your customers, how you construct your business, and the levers you can use to differentiate and create value all can change with a services focus. This is a foundational concept of Open Services Innovation and the topic examined in detail in this chapter. The subsequent chapters in Part One develop each of the other implications in depth.

DEFINING *SERVICES*

Let's start by defining what is meant by *services*. As I noted in the Introduction, many services are becoming quite knowledge intensive, and these are the ones that offer the greatest opportunity for new business growth. Since *services* means different things to different people, I begin by clarifying what I mean by the term in this book.

The origin of the term *services* in English derives from the Latin *servitium*, meaning "slavery." The related word *servant* has a similar derivation.[1] The root of the word has far-reaching implications in both the West and in Asia. In the West, "services" often connotes a low-status work activity, and in Asia, the term has perhaps an even more menial association. A variety of activities that fall under the traditional use of the word *service* suggest why this is so. A haircut at the local barber and a personal service such as a manicure or a massage are activities that seem unlikely to hold the key to advancing economic prosperity in a postmanufacturing economy.

A different definition of the term *services*, however, points toward a more prosperous future. It comes not from Latin but from some government economists working in the United States in the early twentieth century. The modern use of the term *services* arose from a taxonomy of the U.S. economy that dates to the 1930s from the Department of Commerce.[2] In the Standard Industrial Classification taxonomy, the major economic sectors were agriculture, manufacturing, and services. This reflected the dominant economic activity of the time, which was experiencing a shift from an agricultural to a manufacturing economy. In this taxonomy, according to one of the most influential scholars, the term *services* refers to "a change in the condition of a person, or a good belonging to some economic entity, brought about as the result of the activity of some other economic entity, with the approval of the first person or economic entity."[3]

The U.S. government uses this definition as the basis for defining service products in the North American Product Classification System.[4] Services in recent years have become more knowledge intensive and have been increasingly able to harness knowledge in improving their effectiveness, quality, and variety.

An analysis of this definition and others like it shows that services activities differ in important ways from product activities. In a product exchange, products are a means to a desired end rather than the end itself. After the product exchange takes place, the product provider's job is done. It is then the customer's responsibility to use that product to reach the desired end. In a service exchange, the services provider's task is not finished until the customer's need is fulfilled.[5] Customers often desire to have their needs fulfilled not only initially but over a series of interactions with their provider. This shift requires companies now to think about the lifetime value of their customers across many transactions. It then stimulates them to learn more about their customers so that their knowledge of their customers' needs also grows over time. It can even motivate companies to craft more customized or personalized solutions for their customers, driving up satisfaction, reducing customer switching to competitors, and capturing more value from more satisfied customers.

DEFINING YOUR BUSINESS

In thinking about your business as a service, consider the classic formulation of a business as a chain of economic activities that adds value to a product. Michael Porter's classic book, *Competitive Advantage,* identifies this value chain as a powerful tool for conceptualizing businesses and how to innovate them.[6] It has been widely taught in business schools around the world, is installed in the operating procedures of myriad companies as well, and frames the way people think about their business. So it is worth taking another look at it (see Figure 2.1).

The action moves in the figure from the left to the right, in the direction of the arrow. Inputs come in on the left and are transformed into outputs through the processes detailed in the figure. Some of the processes are core manufacturing activities (inbound logistics, operations, and outbound logistics), and others are supporting activities (human resources, technology development, and procurement).

Notice that the product is the star in this figure. Service does not appear until the very end of the process, just before the product gets to the customer. Some service is delivered to the customer as part of the sale (such as installation), but the lion's share of it is delivered after the sale in this approach. So service is conceived as the end of the process, to "finish" the product's sale or keep the product operating once it is purchased. This

FIGURE 2.1   Porter's Product-Driven Business Model

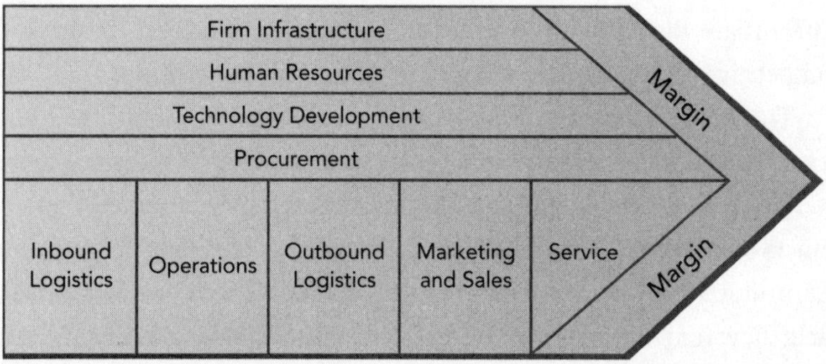

Source: Reprinted with the permission of Free Press, a Division of Simon & Schuster, Inc., from COMPETITIVE ADVANTAGE: Creating and Sustaining Superior Performance by Michael E. Porter. Copyright © 1985, 1998 by Michael E. Porter. All rights reserved.

reflects the mind-set of many executives toward their business today, more than twenty-five years after the model was developed: that the important stuff happens with the product. This is a product-focused approach to thinking about your business.

An example of Porter's value chain might be manufacturing an automobile. The automotive company must procure steel, glass, electronics, and other items, which its operations turn into a vehicle. That vehicle must then be accessorized, painted, and shipped to a dealer. The customer purchases the vehicle from the dealer, who readies the car for the customer to drive off the lot. The customer then comes back periodically to the dealer for maintenance. These after-sale services are provided so that the customer will buy the product, but they are not core to the business. Competitive advantage in this model thus comes from having better products, or differentiated products, or the lowest-cost products—not better services for them.

Services in the product-based approach to business reflected in the Porter model are something of an afterthought. To stay with the automotive example, car companies don't even provide service. Instead it is outsourced to auto dealers, which are at the end of Porter's value chain, with only limited ability to suit the customer's desires. The service function itself is typically run as a cost center, and the people in the service organization are not the fast-track managers destined for the top of the organization someday. Instead the services area is something of an organizational backwater: a necessary function but not something to differentiate the company and lead to competitive success. Little or no competitive advantage arises from services in this conception.

This view dominates the way most companies think about their businesses today. Nevertheless, some important contrary voices have been overlooked. Marketing guru Ted Levitt has famously observed that customers often want not the product itself but rather the effect that the product produces. In his example, customers do not want to buy a power drill itself; they want the holes that the drill will make. Peter Drucker made much the same observation: "What the customer buys and considers value is never a product. It is always utility—that is, what a product does for him."[7]

Thinking about your business as a service business requires moving away from Porter's value chain and following instead the alternative logic of Levitt and Drucker. In a service approach to automobiles, the chain must be replaced. This approach would not conceive of the car as a transaction, highlighted by the purchase of the vehicle. Rather, it would think of the car as a delivery method for providing transportation as a service over a period of time. A services view might conceive of the offering as "transportation services" or "mobility services" or even "transportation experiences." Thus, no single purchase activity provides the climax to the process or an end to the relationship; instead, there needs to be a series of ongoing interactions with the customer over time. Figure 2.2 provides a graphical representation of this alternative way of thinking.

Notice in Figure 2.2 that there are still inputs, processes, and outputs. But these are no longer interacting exclusively with internal support functions. Instead, they also interact with customers (Customer Co-Creation); with external sources of ideas, technologies, and services (Open Innovation); and even attract third-party investment and support

FIGURE 2.2   Open Services Value Chain

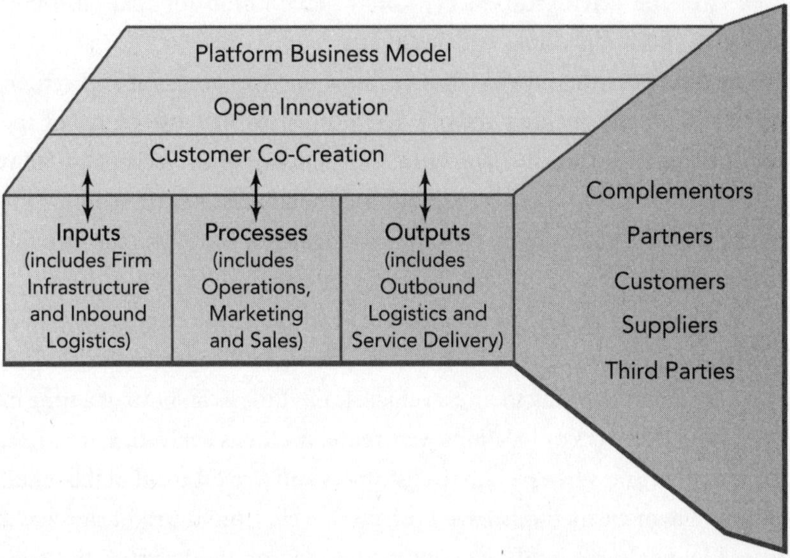

Platform Business Model

Open Innovation

Customer Co-Creation

Inputs (includes Firm Infrastructure and Inbound Logistics)	Processes (includes Operations, Marketing and Sales)	Outputs (includes Outbound Logistics and Service Delivery)

Complementors

Partners

Customers

Suppliers

Third Parties

(Platform Business Model). As the services value chain goes to market, the offering does not come to a single point; rather, it widens to incorporate the activities and offerings of many other parties as part of going to market. Indeed, open innovation and services are at the core of this model.

To return to the automotive example, if the customer were freed from having to own a vehicle, different vehicles could be provided at different times based on the type of transportation the customer wanted or needed. If a variety of providers worked together, perhaps a transportation services provider could create a platform for delivering a variety of experiences or expanded utility to a single customer. With this approach, the customer could choose from an array of possibilities, depending on whether he or she wanted to drive around town, take a long road trip, go off-road into the mountains, haul some cargo, or have an elegant night on the town.

To extend this alternative approach a bit further, imagine that each customer had a key that could access one of the vehicles of a transportation services provider. The customer's prior preferences, driving habits, behaviors, and characteristics (favorite radio stations, preferred cabin temperature, and seat position, for example) would be contained in this key. So even when the customer was using a different vehicle, certain aspects of the driving experience could be common for that customer across the fleet of possible vehicle choices.

In a services-driven view of a business, services are front and center. They are a profit-making activity (in contrast to the cost center of the product-based view) and are used to differentiate the company from its competitors. The people running the function are at the core of the business and are as important as the product people for future leadership in the organization.

A growing variety of automotive transportation service business models take a new approach, as do the older ones like taxis. Some are as new as the Zipcar, a way to hire a vehicle for as little as an hour at a time in increasing numbers of locations. Car rental itself has evolved; Enterprise, for example, offers free pickup to customers and free drop-off of the rental vehicle. Payment methods have evolved as well, from outright purchase, to car loans, leases, and payment by the day or the hour or the trip. Table 2.1 shows how a few of these approaches vary on six dimensions.

TABLE 2.1 Services-Based View of Transportation Services

	Selection of Vehicle	Delivery of Vehicle	Maintenance of Vehicle	Information and Training	Payment and Financing	Protection and Insurance
Car purchase or lease (product-focused approach)	Customer chooses	Customer picks from dealer stock	Customer does this	Customer does this	Customer, dealer, or third party	Customer provides
Taxi	Supplier chooses	Customer is picked up	Supplier does this	Supplier does this	By the ride, based on time and distance	Supplier provides
Enterprise car rental	Customer chooses from local stock	Customer picks up or is picked up	Supplier does this	Supplier does this	By the day	Customer is responsible
Zipcar	Customer chooses from local stock	From Zipcar locations	Supplier does this	Supplier does this	By the hour	Customer purchases from supplier

This comparison makes it clear that a services business model looks at cars very differently from a product-based model. Sometimes the customer selects the vehicle, but other times the transportation services provider selects the vehicle and the customer simply receives the transportation service. The maintenance of the vehicle varies by the chosen mode of transportation services. How payment is made differs widely as well, from outright acquisition of a vehicle over its useful life, to renting an hour's use or a single trip in the vehicle. The insurance protection for the vehicle is bundled in with some modes of transportation services and broken out separately in others. In sum, Table 2.1 shows how different approaches to a services business invoke different combinations of business processes.

THE UTILIZATION DIFFERENTIAL

Looking at these different forms of car transportation services leads to the realization of a less easily observed factor that plays a major role in converting product-based business approaches to services-based businesses: the utilization differential. Managing utilization is an often overlooked method to reduce fixed costs, increase profitability, and drive a higher return on investment. By utilizing an asset more effectively, a transportation services provider can provide better service to a customer at a price at or below what the customer herself would pay, while still making money itself.

Utilization is the concept of how frequently an asset (in this case, a car) is used. Most people in the United States own their cars and drive them ten thousand to twelve thousand miles per year. If they average a speed of 30 miles per hour (balancing highway driving with city driving and other local trips), that represents 333 to 400 hours of driving per year. But there are 24 hours in a day and 365 days in a year, so the total available time to use the car each year is 8,760 hours. This means that the typical driver is driving his or her car about 3.8 to 4.6 percent of the time. The rest of the time, the car is not being driven. And of course the owner is solely responsible for all of the maintenance, insurance, parking, and other costs of the vehicle.

By comparison, consider a taxi. Many taxis are company owned, with more than one driver driving the taxi each day, taking turns on different shifts. A taxi might be used for 22 hours or more each day (allowing some time for changing drivers and returning to base, for example). That taxi might be driven for all but a few days per year (those days off would be for scheduled maintenance). Under these assumptions, such a taxi would be used 22 hours a day, 360 days a year, for 7,920 hours each year, for more than 90 percent utilization of the vehicle. Admittedly the taxi would not be driving passengers all of that time because of gaps between dropping off one customer and picking up another. But the car is nevertheless available for hire, with a driver, for 90 percent of the hours during the year.

The utilization differential is the difference between the personal utilization of 3.8 to 4.6 percent, in comparison to the up to 90 percent utilization of the taxi. This is a difference of a factor of twenty or more in this instance. It means that the fixed costs of the car (the purchase price, but also the maintenance, license fees, the insurance, and other expenses) can be spread over many, many more hours by a service provider (the taxi service) relative to a car purchased as a product for personal use.

Particular services-based approaches to transportation can provide other benefits for customers. Parking in urban locations, for example, can be quite expensive, and avoiding that expense and hassle is worth a lot. Vehicle maintenance is an inconvenience at best and a time-consuming frustration at worst. These are hidden costs that many customers do not consider when purchasing a new vehicle. They add to the total cost of providing transportation services themselves by buying the car. They also reflect the myopia that can arise from an overly product-focused view of transportation. By leveraging a utilization differential, transportation services providers could develop new services that address these hidden costs that many customers may have. The key idea here is that understanding all of a customer's costs is an important way to take advantage of the utilization differential. By making more effective use of an underutilized asset, you can develop new ways to save customers time and money while making more profit for yourself.

Such a large utilization differential creates opportunities for services providers to offer services at attractive prices to consumers, while still being able to profit from higher utilization of the product that delivers the service. This is true for physical assets of many kinds, such as business jets (for example, think of NetJets, which offers fractional jet ownership to its customers), computer servers (IBM managing your data on its servers rather than your own), copiers (Xerox delivering copies from its copiers rather than you doing so on your own), buildings (real estate investment trusts often buy and lease back corporate office space to the owner), and even sailboats (we examine a sailing club in Chapter Seven). It extends to business assets of many kinds, including intellectual property and brands. These are all important ways in which a services focus toward a business can unlock new sources of valuable growth.

The ability to get more out of assets by increased utilization is a powerful profit driver for businesses. As we will see, allowing others to use your assets for their business requirements (another way to improve asset utilization) may provide even further savings and profitability for your business.

A PRODUCTS VERSUS SERVICES APPROACH

The utilization differential is one example of a source of value from rethinking the transportation business as a service rather than from a product perspective. Services businesses can also find new sources of growth from rethinking their business. One of the most dramatic examples of this comes from the food industry.[8]

The Food Industry

Food is a universal commodity that we all understand. But people experience food in a variety of ways, and consumers make a range of services choices in consuming food. These have different business models. Some are close to the traditional product-driven approach, and others are a strongly services-driven view.

Customers have many needs when it comes to food. At the most basic level, we want food for basic sustenance and nutrition. We want to spend as little as necessary, since we consume two or three meals a day each day of the year (food is 5 to 25 percent of the average household's budget). But there is more to food than being a source of nutrition that is cheap in cost.

Food is also an experience. We want it to be tasty, and we want our kids, guests, and significant others to eat it, so they must decide that it tastes good. Note that tastes differ: what a six-year-old child thinks is good differs markedly from what a college student prefers, which differs from the typical professional, which differs from the typical retiree. So it is not always a simple matter to serve food that tastes good to a diverse group of people at a reasonable cost. As with autos, the customer faces a range of choices in how nutritional products and services are obtained. Customers can buy the food and prepare it themselves. Or they can choose from a range of experiences in which someone else prepares the food. To examine this, we turn to a comparison of the chef versus the grocer.

The Product-Focused Grocery Business

Both the chef and the grocer are services that provide food, but they do so in very different ways (Table 2.2 summarizes the comparison). While retailing groceries is technically a services business, the grocer follows a rather product-focused approach. The grocer sells the ingredients and accompanying items for meals. The grocer works very hard to get food that is fresh, low cost, well displayed, and in stock when customers want it. The customers of the grocer, however, must take it on themselves to perform all of the additional tasks of turning a list of grocery items into one or more meals. Basically the customer buys a number of products and turns those products into meals. This is like purchasing the vehicle: customers buy the products, insurance, fuel, parking, and so on in order to obtain transportation services.

Customers then perform the key integration tasks for this service of serving food. They have a recipe in mind for what food is to be served; how that food is to be prepared; cutting, trimming, cleaning, and otherwise preparing the food for cooking; cooking the food (and trying to arrange it

TABLE 2.2   The Grocer and the Chef: A Comparison

	Grocer	Chef
Building blocks	Food, drink	Food, drink
Who performs the integration	Customer	Chef, staff, and servers
Hidden costs	Food preparation, cleaning tableware, cleanup, washing, putting leftover food away	None (with the exception of not knowing what is in the prepared food)
Relevant capital equipment	Kitchen, tableware	Facility, parking, kitchen, tableware

so that multiple courses are ready at roughly the same time); and serving the food.

There are a lot of hidden costs in doing all this that are not reflected in the prices paid at the grocery checkout counter. The pots and pans must be (at least relatively) clean. So too the dishes, cups, and silverware that will serve the meal. The stove, oven, grill, and other cooking devices must be ready for use. The table must be set. Then everything has to be cleaned up, and the leftover ingredients and food put away for later use. In addition to these hidden costs in converting food into a meal, the capital equipment for making the meal is the responsibility of the customer, not the grocer (see Table 2.2).

The Services Approach in the Food Business

Compare this product approach of the grocer to the chef. The advent of restaurants is a relatively recent historical development. Aside from royalty and the nobility, most households throughout most of recorded human history have had to prepare their own food. The idea of an industry catering to the food needs of a broad mass of society came into being only after the Industrial Revolution.[9]

Restaurants are a decidedly different option for obtaining nutrition. Businesses that seek to provide meals to customers must work hard to attract customers and differentiate their businesses from one another. As Table 2.2 shows, a chef's business must also include a variety of additional assets that the grocer does not have to worry about.

Customers are offered a set of choices of food to order, along with drinks to accompany the meal. But the integration task for shopping for, preparing, and serving this meal is entrusted entirely to the chef (and staff, if any). The chef has already preselected the menu of choices to be offered, and the shopping for the ingredients to create these choices has already been done. The recipes for preparing the food are in the mind of the chef and may be completely unknown to the customer. The order of arrival of food, the presentation of the food, and the dishes, glasses, silverware, and other makings of a meal are all provided by the chef for the customer. The chef (or staff) takes care of clearing the table, putting the leftover ingredients away, and so forth. Many of the hidden costs for the product-based view of obtaining nutrition through grocery shopping are therefore taken care of for the customer.

More subtly, the setting in which the food is consumed is also a concern for the chef. The proper venue is an important part of the experience of enjoying the food. This extends to how many tables to provide, how close together to place the tables, whether air-conditioning is used, and at what temperature the drinks are served. These are concerns that do not trouble the grocer.

The Business Model in Services Versus Product Approaches

The experience of a meal thus can be delivered through two quite different approaches. In one, the customer takes on the integration responsibilities and bears a number of hidden costs. In the other, the provider takes on the integration tasks and the hidden costs as well as the direct costs of the food. In other words, the grocer sells the building blocks (from the customer's view), while the chef sells a total solution.

Another way to contrast the grocer and the chef is to revisit Porter's value chain and examine how the two businesses transform their inputs into outputs for the customer. Note that the business as I have defined it differs markedly between the two approaches, even though the result is still a meal. The target market is different: the grocer is aiming for a high-volume mass market. The value proposition is the food you want in the quantity you want it, at a great price. The key to this market is to have items that most customers will want and sell them all before they perish or expire. Cost and availability are vital, as is knowing what to stock, how to display it, and how to get customers in and out of the store rapidly. Therefore, working with suppliers is critical to delivering the value proposition. Suppliers must have the capability to respond rapidly to changes in orders from the store and provide the supplies at very competitive prices.

Openness is also key to grocers. Grocery stores must be rather open to perform these feats. They share their customer purchase data with all of their key suppliers, and devise reordering rules with their suppliers to keep the products they need in stock. Many grocers have now given control over their most precious asset, their shelf space on the floor of the store, to their key suppliers. These key suppliers manage the information, the pricing, the merchandising, and the reordering to maximize the value of the shelf space in that store. Many grocers are now also inviting other services onto their premises, such as bank ATM machines, coffee kiosks, video rental kiosks, and others. These seemingly unrelated services provide additional convenience to customers (one-stop shopping, which we discuss more in Chapter Four) and additional revenue streams to the grocer. Table 2.3 details this comparison.

Now consider the business of the chef. The chef is delivering an experience to the customer. He or she has restricted the customer's choice to a preselected set of options. The value proposition is that of a complete meal, ready to eat, which implies convenience and satisfaction. The chef also must make a critical choice of what market segment in the food industry to serve. It is a truism that one type of chef or restaurant cannot serve the entire market. A luxurious meal at a Michelin-starred restaurant is very different from that of a quick bite at a fast food joint. A diner caters to a different customer than a cafeteria does. And even within a single kind of restaurant, such as fast food, a plethora of different segments is

TABLE 2.3   Comparing the Grocer and Chef Business Models

	Grocer	Chef
Target market	Consumers	Diners
Value proposition	Wide selection, quality, price	Dining experience
Core elements	Rapid inventory turns, choosing correct merchandise	Great food, skilled cooks, atmosphere
Value chain	Food suppliers, related items, logistics, information technology, distribution centers	Fresh produce, local ingredients, quality equipment, knowledgeable and courteous servers
Revenue mechanism	Small markup over cost, very high volume, rapid inventory turns	High markups over cost, low volume, alcohol, tips
Value network, ecosystem	Other services on premises, parking	Cookbooks, parking, special events

served, from burgers to Mexican, to Chinese or a deli, from sit-down to takeout, and even home delivery.

Openness matters to the chef as well, but it is openness of a different character from that of the grocer. Chefs, for example, often build their reputations by publishing books of their recipes. They are also sharing more information with customers about the ingredients used in their food, either by choice or by regulatory requirement. Although chefs are openly sharing their knowledge, it is the sharing of an expert, imparting tacit knowledge and experience to someone not trained in the craft. Some restaurants are even opening cooking schools in their facilities (typically in the slow periods of the day, thus leveraging the utilization advantage) to impart some of this tacit knowledge.

El Bulli: The Restaurant as a Platform

To bring the grocer and chef comparison into reality, consider the world-renowned restaurant El Bulli.[10] Based in the Catalonian province of Spain,

El Bulli is widely considered one of the world's best and most influential restaurants. *Restaurant Magazine* voted the restaurant number 1 in the world four times, and the restaurant received its third Michelin star in 1997 and has held it ever since. Don't rush to book a reservation, though. The restaurant receives roughly 1 million requests for its eight thousand seatings each year (it closes for six months each year for research and development), and reservations are typically taken on a single day in October for the coming year. And the restaurant is planning to close for the years 2011 and 2012, though its research activities (see below) will continue during that time.

The restaurant and its chef, Ferran Adrià, are best known for investigations into "molecular gastronomy." By examining the microproperties of specific foods, spices, and ingredients, Adrià develops unique recipes that provide radically new dining experiences. This knowledge did not originate inside El Bulli. Adrià was among the eager collaborators of a series of discoveries in molecular gastronomy by Hervé This, a French physical chemist. El Bulli was also a participant in a European Union–funded project, INICON, that intended to promote collaboration among scientists, chefs, and restaurants. Although El Bulli has made important contributions to this movement, the core ideas initially emerged outside the organization and were then absorbed inside. Recently the School of Engineering and Applied Sciences at Harvard University agreed to bring scientific expertise and techniques in the formulation of foods, textures, and structures to El Bulli as well, so this pattern of importing scientific insights and translating them into delicious cuisine is likely to continue.

Although El Bulli's gastronomy is widely celebrated, its approach to its business is much less celebrated. As noted, the restaurant closes for six months every year and reportedly loses money. In contrast, most three-star Michelin restaurants seek to sell as many dinners over as many nights as they can (think back to the utilization advantage). However, the restaurant's role in El Bulli's model is one of an R&D laboratory, which is not expected to earn a profit by itself. Instead, the restaurant generates the knowledge needed for the profitable elements of El Bulli's business.

Most of these elements provide profitable ways for others to share the restaurant's resources, including its brand and its knowledge. So the restaurant loses money but creates the knowledge and insight that fuel these other elements of it. To think of it another way, the restaurant serves as the platform on which a number of ancillary business activities are developed.

In 1999 the restaurant decided to share its knowledge with the food manufacturer Borges to design oils, sauces, and snacks. Borges's series of co-branded items with El Bulli in the consumer marketplace added a new revenue stream for El Bulli and provided Borges with an important differentiation in its markets. Other similar co-branding deals for El Bulli included collaborations with Kaiku (an award-winning book of recipes), Lavazza (coffee), NH Hoteles (hospitality), Nestlé (chocolate), Armand Basi (tableware and kitchenware), and Diageo (whisky cocktails). In another area, a recent collaboration was launched between NH Hoteles and Iberia airline in 2007 to include Fast Good sandwiches in the menu on Iberia flights. This benefited El Bulli by positioning its brand into a new segment of customers who previously were underserved by the elegant, expensive restaurant.

This last relationship between NH Hoteles and El Bulli deserves further comment. In order to reinforce the brand experience of its customers and position itself in the market as an innovative organization, NH Hoteles decided to create the concept of Fast Good, a fast food restaurant delivering food of better quality, and Nhube, an initiative that seeks to combine different elements in a single space: the lounge, the restaurant, and the café-bar of the hotels. To complete these projects, NH Hoteles decided to rely on the capabilities and resources of the restaurant El Bulli and its proprietor, Adrià. Through the cooperation with El Bulli, NH Hoteles was granted access to resources such as El Bulli's expertise in creating brand experiences and the El Bulli brand itself, which reinforced the positioning of NH Hoteles as an innovative brand.

The co-branding path of El Bulli, based on a few deep, specific partnerships, seeks to maintain control over the El Bulli brand. This control helps to prevent overexposure of the brand, which degrades its value, as arguably has happened with brands like Yves Saint Laurent and Calvin Klein. El Bulli restaurant prefers deep relationships with a few selected partners because one of the resources it shares is process technology, which is difficult to protect legally.

El Bulli shows just what a creative rethinking of a service business can do to generate new business models. A restaurant that closes for half of every year has enabled its proprietor to contribute to a much wider variety of businesses on top of his own. This makes El Bulli a restaurant but also a brand and a platform for new business creation. If this can be achieved in the very mature restaurant industry, imagine what platforms might be erected in more dynamic services settings.

Services in the Semiconductor Industry

For another example of a services approach to business, this one in a more technologically advanced industry, we turn to the Taiwan Semiconductor Manufacturing Corporation (TSMC).[11]

TSMC is perhaps the most important company in Taiwan, yet very few people have heard of it. It makes a thriving business selling services to other businesses, which in turn sell the products that result from these services to customers. For those who know the business of semiconductors, TSMC is rightly celebrated as the pioneer of a new model for making semiconductor chips. Figure 2.3 illustrates this new model.

Long ago the only companies that made semiconductor chips were companies like AT&T and IBM that also designed the systems that used those chips. There were no standards for chip design in those days, and scientists had to know the systems intimately in order to design chips to use in those systems. As technology advanced, start-up companies like Intel offered chips as replacements for the memory in IBM systems, which led to the new integrated device manufacturer (IDM) model. With the IDM model, there was no longer a need to design the entire system in order to design better chips for use in that system. This model made it possible for companies like Intel to provide these products.

This model continued through the 1970s and the 1980s, when a new model began to emerge in the semiconductor business. As it happens, this new model, called the foundry model, was a services model that TSMC

FIGURE 2.3   Evolution of the Semiconductor Business Model

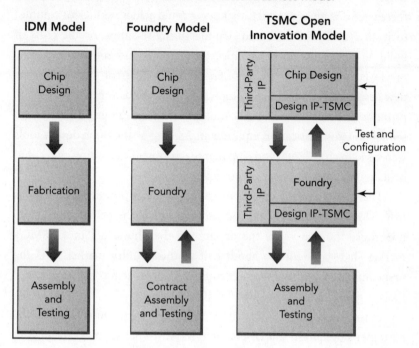

pioneered. TSMC provided manufacturing services from its manufacturing facilities (foundries) to its clients, who designed new semiconductor chips. The customers took these designs to TSMC, and TSMC fabricated the designs onto silicon wafers and gave these back to its customers. The customers then packaged them into individual chips and sold them. So TSMC's customers did not have to invest in expensive manufacturing plants (called *fabs* in industry parlance) to create and sell chips. These TSMC customers were called "fabless semiconductor companies." Instead, they relied on TSMC to do the fabrication work for them.

The fabless semiconductor model emerged from the efforts of Morris Chang and his colleagues who founded TSMC. They were supported by extensive government assistance in Taiwan and the talents of a centralized government research lab, ITRI. Chang was a veteran of Silicon Valley and knew well the economics of the semiconductor business. He knew that for every high-volume product success like the Intel microprocessor, there were dozens of products that never could achieve sufficient volumes to justify their own dedicated manufacturing facilities. As the costs of building new fabrication facilities grew, more and more companies' products would have to be manufactured in a different way. Moreover, new design methodologies and tools from independent firms offered the promise of being able to build multiple product designs on the same semiconductor fabrication equipment. As long as the same design tools were used in chip design and chip manufacturing, the resulting chip could be manufactured on TSMC's equipment.[12]

This is a high-tech variant of co-creation. Chip designers use tools from TSMC and independent companies to design their chips, and TSMC uses those tools to verify the design and then build it. Since TSMC's market share amounts to about half of the foundry market, it is the first company for which supplier companies build semiconductor design tools, a significant advantage to TSMC.

In the beginning, TSMC simply performed the manufacturing of the customer's design. In this co-creation, the customer supplied the design, and TSMC performed the manufacturing. Soon, though, TSMC learned to impose certain design restrictions on its customers so that the designs would conform to the requirements of TSMC's manufacturing processes. These early design restrictions were housed largely inside TSMC.

But recently TSMC has gone further to develop an even stronger position. As the foundry market begins to mature and competitors improve their own foundry capabilities, TSMC has decided to develop a new service that it calls its Open Innovation Platform. Here is a helpful description from a Gartner analyst:

> [The] Open Innovation Platform (OIP) is a program that involves more "collaboration between the foundry and its clients at the early stages of the design phase," said Jim Walker, an analyst with Gartner, in Gartner's e-mail newsletter. TSMC's OIP consists of a platform of design tools and IP [intellectual property] to help customers with their design-to-manufacturing efforts. OIP integrates TSMC's manufacturing technologies, silicon IP, massive manufacturing database and compatible

third-party silicon IP and design tools. Through OIP, TSMC can offer vertically integrated services, from designing and manufacturing to testing and packaging, thus shortening clients' IC [integrated circuit] development processes and reducing their manufacturing costs.[13]

With the growth of TSMC's business ecosystem, many other third-party companies that made design tools, process recipes, testing, and packaging all began to take steps to assure their customers that their offerings would run on TSMC's processes. By being such a large factor in the foundry market, TSMC became the de facto standard for all third parties to develop for. This explosion in third-party offerings creates more design options for TSMC's customers, a clear benefit. However, these offerings also increase the complexity for TSMC's customers to manage, and this complexity risks causing new chips to require redesigns or other expensive modifications to be manufactured correctly.

TSMC's Open Innovation Platform addresses this increased complexity by providing a new level of integration and coordination. By offering its own design and manufacturing services and services from many third-party companies, and then testing these all together, TSMC has constructed a platform. TSMC now provides documented interfaces for its manufacturing processes to its ecosystem, so that these third parties can be confident that their offerings will comply with TSMC's process requirements and will join the platform as well. With compliant offerings that conform to these interfaces, TSMC tests and then certifies to customers of those offerings that they can use these tools with confidence that the chip will turn out properly the first time through the process. TSMC's Open Innovation Platform helps its customers get their designs manufactured on the first pass. This avoids expensive turns of the chip design, whereby the chip must be redesigned in order to be manufactured correctly in volume. The result is faster time to market for TSMC's customers and at a lower cost of design.

TSMC's Open Innovation Platform also raises a topic area that has not been discussed much in this book so far: intellectual property (IP). It is commonly believed that services businesses cannot benefit much from IP because patents are relatively less commonly used in services. The

TSMC example shows how IP can create and capture value in a services context (and the previous example of El Bulli shows the ability to capture value from another form of IP, trademarks, as well). By developing its own IP for designing and verifying chips for its customers and creating published interfaces and validation for third-party design IP, TSMC can lock its foundry customers into its own internal fab services. By providing the assurance that conforming products will work the first time through the fab facility, TSMC removes some of the anxiety and risk its customers face. It stands as a powerful example of co-creation, in this case giving customers more tools to design better chips, with the assurance that the design will work the first time through the process. We examine co-creation more in the next chapter.

Both of these features—TSMC's own IP and assurance programs— also raise the bar for TSMC competitors, making it harder to unseat TSMC as the foundry of choice. While the Open Innovation Platform has been in existence for only a short time as of this writing, it is likely to cement TSMC's position as the market leader in the foundry business.

TSMC's Open Innovation Platform thus raises another concept: open innovation in services. TSMC does not provide all of the services itself. Rather, it benefits from incorporating external IP provided by others, along with internal IP it generated, and then certifying the resulting pieces for its customers. This invites an analysis of the role of open innovation in services, the topic of Chapter Four in this book.

o o o

We have come a long way from the product-dominant thinking of the traditional value chain. As our economy moves more toward services, our thinking must keep pace. Services provide experiences for customers, and these experiences provide chances to differentiate and grow the business. Whether it is the low-tech food industry or the advanced-technology semiconductor industry, services are providing a critical edge to market leaders over their competitors.

In the next chapter, we take the idea of customer experiences further by inviting customers directly into the innovation process.

CHAPTER 3

CO-CREATE WITH YOUR CUSTOMERS

This chapter builds on the changes that businesses experience when they frame their business as a service. It specifically examines co-creation and shows how involving your customers in your own innovation activities can bring greater value to them and greater competitive advantage for you.

THE CHANGING ROLE OF CUSTOMERS IN SERVICES

Product businesses think of customers as consumers at the end of the value chain. They design products based on their research into what their consumers want and are willing to pay for and engage in their development processes. Consumers then receive the output.

In the world of products, suppliers develop specifications to describe the product to potential customers. Customers can compare specifications of alternative product options to find the right product for their needs. Suppliers need not know exactly what the customer intends to do with the product, so long as those products meet the specs. Customers in turn do not have to spell out their intentions and plans; they can simply evaluate the specs and test products to verify that the product does in fact meet the specification claimed by the manufacturer.[1] In many cases, the resulting spec is one that averages out the input from a variety of different customers, such that no one customer is offered exactly what he or she asked for, but instead must be content with those specs that are common to other customers as well.

When you think of your business as a service (whether you are making a product or providing a service), you think of your customers differently. Their role in the innovation process changes.

In the world of services, it is much harder to develop specifications than it is in the world of products. It is harder for customers to compare specifications on an apples-for-apples basis and harder as well to verify that the specifications claimed are in fact being delivered by the supplier. Often customers need to explain more about what they need in the way of services, and their needs likely vary from one organization to another. Suppliers in turn can no longer dedicate themselves to long production runs and one-size-fits-all thinking to serve these customers. Instead they have to figure out how to give the customer what the customer needs, while also figuring out a way to do this profitably for themselves. This change introduces a tension between standardization, which makes providing the service more cost-effective for the supplier, and customization, which more closely matches the customer's needs but may require different solutions for each customer.

TACIT KNOWLEDGE

The tension between standardization and customization is due to the fact that much of the knowledge involved in providing or buying services is tacit, that is, gained from experience. It is both difficult and expensive to write down this knowledge. Customers vary in their prior experiences, and suppliers vary in their prior activities as well. Tacit knowledge interferes with the ability of suppliers and customers to communicate with one another.[2] It can be very difficult for a supplier to understand what a customer really wants.

Examples of Tacit Knowledge

A classic example of tacit knowledge is learning to ride a bicycle.[3] From my own parenting experience of two children, I can personally vouch for the difficulty in transferring such knowledge. For most physical challenges children undertake, going slower reduces the chance of an accident and reduces the amount of pain from any accident they do have (think of running, jumping, or tumbling). With bicycling, the fundamental—and counterintuitive—insight is that the centripetal force that keeps a bicycle upright is stronger when the rider is going faster. The rider, in order to avoid falling, must go faster, in contravention of her initial instincts. This must be experienced in order to be believed—at least if my children are at all typical of this learning process!

The FedEx package tracking system described in Chapter One demonstrates one way to deal with tacit information: let the customers themselves provide the information directly. By opening its system directly to its customers without any intermediary, FedEx eliminates the potential for confusion, misunderstanding, or misinterpretation of the customer's wishes. Should the customer make a mistake in entering the information, he has only himself to blame.

There are further benefits. Customers have more control: they can use FedEx's services in whatever ways at whatever times they wish. They can change their own processes as a result of being able to access FedEx's service. They get all the information they want, whenever they want it, and it is accurate. Administrative support staffs of many organizations have learned to trust this system and become quite skilled in using it. So a wonderful outcome results for both FedEx and its customers: lower costs, higher satisfaction, and greater customer loyalty.

The Strategic Advantage of Tacit Information

The ability to manage tacit information effectively can create competitive advantage for companies. As computers, networks, and telecommunications move bits around the globe at ever faster speeds, it is precisely the knowledge that doesn't move fast—the tacit knowledge—that becomes increasingly valuable. When customers tell you, rather than everyone else, their tacit needs, you have a unique insight that can help you differentiate yourself in the market. When customers use your systems in ways that they don't use other systems, you have the opportunity to learn from what your customers do that can confer advantage on your business as well.

The FedEx example also shows the important role that information plays in the services sector. Information is both a primary input (the customer enters in the order information to generate the label) and a primary output (the customer learns when the package is delivered) of services activity.

Information technology can play a vital role in accelerating or inhibiting innovation in services if companies are alert to how their customers use their services and keep careful track of this use for future innovations. Consider the following story of how Walmart was able to use its information in stocking its stores in advance of an approaching hurricane to improve service and profits:[4]

> Hurricane Frances was on its way, barreling across the Caribbean, threatening a direct hit on Florida's Atlantic coast.... A week ahead of the storm's landfall, Linda M. Dillman, Wal-Mart's chief information officer, pressed her staff to come up with forecasts based on what had happened when Hurricane Charley struck several weeks earlier. Backed by the trillions of bytes' worth of shopper history that is stored in Wal-Mart's computer network, she felt that the company could "start predicting what's going to happen, instead of waiting for it to happen," as she put it.
>
> The experts mined the data and found that the stores would indeed need certain products—and not just the usual flashlights. "We didn't know in the past that strawberry Pop-Tarts increase in sales, like seven times their normal sales rate, ahead of a hurricane," Ms. Dillman said in a recent interview. "And the pre-hurricane top-selling item was beer."
>
> Thanks to those insights, trucks filled with toaster pastries and six-packs were soon speeding down Interstate 95 toward Wal-Marts in the path of Frances. Most of the products that were stocked for the storm sold quickly, the company said.

By carefully tracking its previous retail experience with its customers in severe storms, Walmart was able to take measures to stock what its customers were likely to want in the next severe weather system—and make more money as a result. Some of these insights were far from obvious. It is perhaps not surprising that flashlights and beer sell well in advance of a possible disaster. But Pop-Tarts? And specifically strawberry-flavored Pop-Tarts? The greater use of information is allowing Walmart to develop a much deeper and more finely grained understanding of its customers.

The more general point is that by collecting and analyzing greater amounts of data, companies can learn from their customers' experiences without having to experience the same context themselves. This creates a powerful opportunity to build competitive advantage into your business by knowing more about your customers than anyone else does. Studying customers' past behaviors allows alert companies to predict their likely future needs, something we see not only with Walmart, but with Google, Amazon, and other firms that carefully collect, analyze, and act on the information they obtain from their customers.

DESIGNING EXPERIENCE POINTS TO FOCUS ON CUSTOMERS

Companies can do more to involve customers in their innovation processes than simply watch them. Some companies, like Lego, headquartered in Denmark, have had great success in letting customers create designs that they would like Lego to produce.[5] An early example of this was Lego Mindstorms, in which Lego included motors with the plastic parts so that consumers could build Lego designs that moved. Someone hacked into the software that came with these motors so that they could make unauthorized modifications to the software and get the Legos to do more. Initially Lego thought that this was illegal (which it was) and should be stopped (which may not have been the right response, as we shall see).

After further thought, Lego reversed course. It opened up its software so that anyone could modify it and watched what customers decided to create. One outcome from this radically open approach was that an entire middle school curriculum was developed to teach children robotics using Legos. Instead of wood shop, where students used saws, planes, drills, and hammers, students were now programming Lego designs to follow a track on the floor or shoot a ball through a basket. Competitions were created in which a set of challenges was given to all competing entrants. The Lego designs best able to accomplish the challenges in the least amount of time won.

More recently, Lego has launched its Architecture line of products. These are Lego kits of some of the leading architectural designs around the world, often created by users. Whether it be Frank Lloyd Wright's Fallingwater, the Empire State building, or the Taj Mahal, Lego has a design for it.

Today Lego's business is growing fastest with adults, a market that did not exist for the company twenty years ago. None of this would ever have happened inside Lego. But this entirely new market was unleashed when Lego let its customers create their own designs, with Lego providing the tools.

Another way for services companies to focus on customers is to create a visualization of the customer's experience. One way to think about a service is to identify its experience points: the moments when a customer comes into direct contact with a service. In services, customers' perceptions of their experiences are as important as the design and delivery of the service. Experience points are opportunities to help frame their expectations of what they will experience. Your customers' satisfaction with your service will be determined by a combination of what you deliver and how that compares to what they expected to receive.

To receive a service, typically customers must make certain choices, and those choices direct them to different elements of the service. A simple example is a restaurant. One experience point is when the customer enters the facility. How is the customer acknowledged? Is he or she greeted in some fashion? Does the customer line up for service, and if so how is that line managed? A second experience point might be when the customer is met by the server. Is there a menu? Are there specials? Is the customer in a hurry (trying to get to a movie or a show, for example), or is it a special occasion where he or she might wish to linger? Still other experience points are shown in Figure 3.1, including the delivery of the food, the dessert and coffee options, the presentation of the bill, the payment process, and parking validation.

FIGURE 3.1   Experience Points in a Restaurant

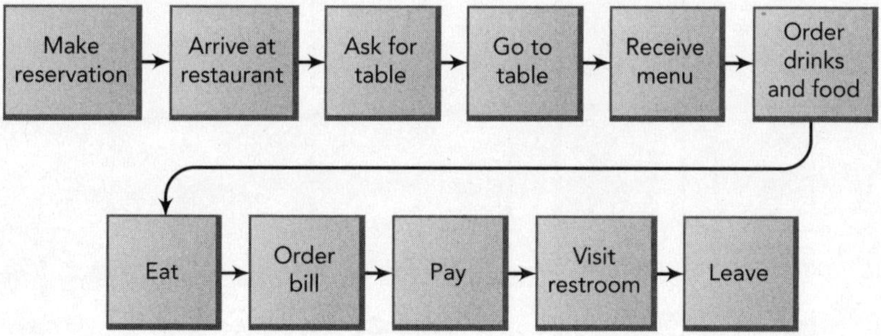

All of these experience points are part of the design of the service, but often we don't see them clearly because services are intangible. Mary Jo Bitner and her colleagues at Arizona State University have developed service blueprinting, a particularly useful visual technique to identify, design, and improve these experience points.[6]

The blueprint starts with a process diagram of the steps that a customer must go through in the course of receiving the service, similar to Figure 3.1. But this tool builds out a richer diagram underneath the experience points, depicting the documents or other artifacts that the customer sees in the process (note that these are tangible), the frontline workers who interact with the customer, the backstage workers who support the process, and the support systems needed to facilitate the process.

In my experience, this technique brings together disparate functional groups that are involved in providing the service. By anchoring the analysis to the customer rather than any particular functional group within the company supplying the service, the technique helps groups overcome the boundaries that often constrain their ability to work together well. In particular, by showing what the customer sees at each step of the process, group members come to understand the role that others play in the process, and how their piece of the process interacts with the rest of the process.

Looking at these experience points in Figure 3.2 takes us beyond Porter's value chain in Figure 2.1. That showed only some of the key value-added steps in the value chain of a (product-based) firm. With this

FIGURE 3.2 Service Blueprint for a Restaurant

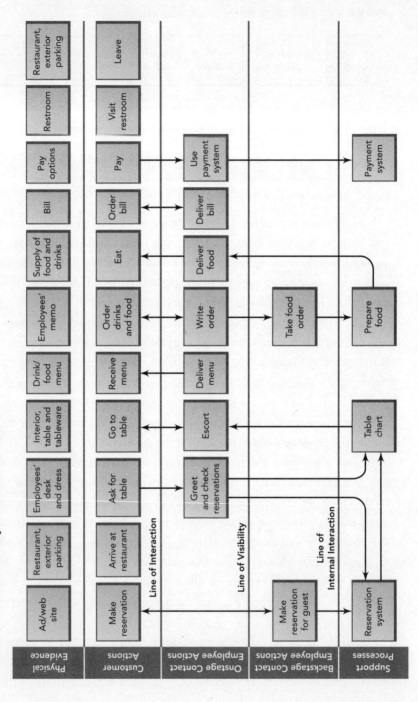

blueprint, we can visualize how the many actions of both customers and employees influence the experience that results from the service. This visualization makes it much easier to spot the root causes of problems and identify ways to improve the service.

LESSONS FROM THE MUSIC INDUSTRY

So far we have looked at single companies involving customers more deeply and more directly in the innovation process. This can be a source of real value for the customers, new revenues for the company, and competitive advantage for the company. But more can be done if we start to consider the power of co-creation across an entire industry. As we shall see, co-creation can revive failing businesses, unleash new markets, and provide far more meaningful experiences to customers. The music industry provides a clear example.

The recorded music industry has experienced tremendous change over the past decade. The sale of CDs is down substantially. Record companies are losing money. Piracy is rampant as many users download music illegally without paying. Legal online delivery channels are selling more songs, but these sales are not enough to compensate for the loss of the CD sales, and margins to the record company are reportedly lower through online channels. In addition, online channels typically sell single tracks rather than entire CDs, so the price point per unit of music sold is much lower as well.

These developments have created a crisis for traditional record companies. Their market is declining, their profits are declining, and how to turn this situation around is far from clear. More fundamentally, the record companies argue, new artists suffer the most from this state of affairs. The online sales channels can sell the work of established artists quite well, but this goes only so far. The Rolling Stones may still be recording new albums when they are in their eighties, for example, but whether anyone will still want to buy them is unknown.

When a business finds itself in serious decline, it is an appropriate time for new thinking and experimentation as well. Knowing that the status quo is no longer sustainable, however, does not identify what to do next. In cases like this, it helps to get back to the customers, the source of value creation in the industry, to determine what can be done to create new, more powerful, more valuable experiences for lots of customers. There are many possible answers, and the best ones are far from obvious at the outset. Instead, one must take risks, run experiments, and pay attention to the results.

One such experiment was done by the alternative music group Radiohead when it launched its most recent album, *In Rainbows,* in fall 2007 with a highly unusual offering to its audience on its Web site. It said, in essence, "Here are the tracks of the new album. Pay us whatever you wish for it." "It's up to you" is the way the site put it. The customer, not the band and certainly not the record company, set the price.

From the perspective of the traditional record company, this was madness. High-quality music available for whatever users wanted to pay was simply an invitation to legal piracy and would destroy any commercial prospects for the album, they said. Worse, some record company executives argued, this experiment devalued music for all artists and was destroying the very fabric of the music business.

That's not quite how it turned out. Some users chose to pay as much as 40 pounds sterling for a special limited-edition version of the album. Many others paid well over retail for the regular CD, and the average price received from the Web sites was $6 for the tracks. More than 1.2 million downloads were made on the first day of the offer. In the end, 38 percent of people paid something and 62 percent paid nothing, according to ComScore.[7]

After two months, Radiohead ended the Web site offer and launched the album into commercial distribution. Although the first week's sales were somewhat below the initial sales of its previous albums, the total commercial sales of *In Rainbows* in its first year of commercial sales was five to six times the sales of the group's previous albums. Part of the reason for the upsurge in commercial sales was that the group earned widespread publicity for its Web site offer and received tremendous play on taste-making sites that influence what other people think is new and hot, like

Last.fm. The promotional push likely caused the group's music to be heard by far more people, in more markets, than any of its previous efforts.

In the end, this was a successful experiment. The band received all of the money directly from its Web site, with no middleman taking a cut. It would have had to sell many times the number of paid downloads it received to have earned an equivalent amount of money. Commercial sales ultimately proved to be quite robust, notwithstanding the early giveaway of its music on the Web site. In addition, the Radiohead tour to promote the album was a huge success, with most venues selling out. The group Coldplay has done a similar experiment. The Grateful Dead has long followed a model of encouraging audiences to tape its music (this was before digital music technology) and made its money from concerts, merchandise, and selling more polished recordings as albums.

The experiment has proven controversial in the music world. The chairman of Def Jam Music Group called the experiment "irresponsible."[8] British songwriter James Blunt thought that the idea was dangerous for artists: "'I don't think they should devalue it,' he told The Times. 'I've got to pay a band and a producer and a mixer. I don't know how I'd necessarily pay them if I sold my albums for 1p [1 pence].'"[9] By contrast, Dominic Howard, the drummer in the popular rock band Muse, took this view of the Radiohead experiment: "This just proves that record companies are becoming more and more useless."[10]

The record companies' argument focuses on these questions:

- How will the next generation of artists find their audience and become established without a recording company to back them?
- Who will invest the money to record them, develop them, promote them, and distribute them in a world saturated with musical offerings of every conceivable type of music?
- How can new artists break through this clutter?

Although the traditional recording company is already a services business, its fundamental mind-set is still that of a product: the creation of the album or CD. Moreover, the innovation process is vertically integrated inside the music company. It is the company that finds the nascent artist or band, invests the money to get the band into the recording studio to cut the tracks of the new product, spends the money and effort to promote the product to the wider world, gets the songs onto playlists at radio stations and TV shows, and sets up interviews with newspapers and magazines to introduce the band to the world.

In this model, consumers are the passive recipients of the music product offered to them. All the work is done for them until they become aware of the new band and start buying the CD. This view of the consumer is a typical mind-set of product-driven businesses. In this view, consumers are freeloaders who will steal if they can, download for free if you let them, and buy the full CD or album only if you manage to withhold it from the online world and force them to go to a store.

Co-Creation: An Alternative Vision for Music

A more services-driven view would invite consumers to be co-creators of their musical journeys. Co-creators are active, engaged seekers of new music, not passive recipients. The bewildering array of online music is not daunting to these co-creators; it is a rich ecosystem full of experiences to be discovered, enjoyed, and shared. Co-creators sample music widely and buy what they like the most. One hot track leads to learning more about the artist and what other tracks this person has. One new style of music leads to finding out who else plays that kind of style. And what your friends are listening to is very important in choosing what you listen to.

Co-creators long to be freed from the tyranny of the CD. A typical CD has ten or twelve tracks, and one or two of them are usually most interesting. With the advent of the digital world, new companies and technologies have arisen to aid in the co-creation process for listeners. Pandora is a company that helps listeners find new music with characteristics similar to the ones that listeners enjoy in the music they currently favor. Once listeners share their preferences with Pandora, Pandora's service pushes new music by other, perhaps unknown, artists that match these characteristics to the listeners to consider. The user's feedback makes Pandora better and better at finding music that is more closely tailored to the listener's interests. Other companies such as BMAT and Last.fm also perform this function.

But co-creators' interests extend beyond simply listening to the music. Another emerging part of the new digital music business is the patronage part of the industry. Patronage companies exploit the fact that some fans are really into certain bands, and their support goes far beyond buying a CD. ArtistShare lets truly committed fans support their chosen bands to a far greater degree than was previously possible in the traditional model. Patrons can receive specialty merchandise from the band. They can get special liner notes or photos of the recording sessions. For the right price, some patrons are invited to attend recording sessions or a release party. Although this model will not scale for millions of listeners, it doesn't need to in order to generate the funds new bands need to get their start. Sellaband is another company that provides a similar patronage model.

Tastemakers: Co-Creating the Promotion of the Music

Once a band gets its start, it needs to begin building an audience. MySpace has become widely known for its many fan pages (filled with tracks, videos, blog postings, fan commentary, and various artwork) linking bands with their audiences.[11] Another young company has developed a new approach to the music business to help address this challenge. Popcuts started in Berkeley, California, in 2008, out of the University of California-Berkeley's School of Information. Popcuts's idea is to craft a model that motivates and rewards trendsetters—the opinion leaders who spot the next new thing before it is widely known. These opinion leaders are also co-creators, because their support for the next new band helps call others' attention to that band. These trendsetters are the secret weapon every band needs to recruit in order to break through the clutter and become well known to a larger audience. They literally co-create the market expansion for new music.

Popcuts recruits, motivates, and rewards these trendsetters by allowing anyone in the general public to buy and download a song (with no digital rights management restricting its distribution). If some other person then buys the same song, the trendsetters who bought it first receive a percentage of that purchase (the amount of the percentage is set by the artist, not by Popcuts). That percentage given to the trendsetter can then be used to buy additional music tracks from Popcuts. And the earlier that someone buys a song, the higher the credit the trendsetter receives. This model is crafted to overcome the inertia of waiting for others to spot new tracks, rewarding tastemakers for early recommendations of songs to others. Popcuts also publicizes its top trendsetters, and new visitors to the Web site often rely on these top trendsetters' recommendations as they search for new music themselves. Amie Street provides a similar service, with additional social networking functions that allow people with similar musical interests to connect with one another. Suurge also provides a trendsetter service capability.

Other parts of the music business are also being reinvented in a more open, services-driven way. Pump Audio connects musicians to producers, to create great sound experiences in the studio. Sonicbids connects musicians to promoters for concerts and gigs. Broadjam.com is a community Web site connecting musicians to one another, as well as to those who can help them advance their careers.

These new companies are mostly small, fledgling organizations. Many will likely not survive over the longer term. But collectively, they sketch out a new, vertically disintegrated approach to the music industry, an approach that engages co-creators proactively in every phase of the music business. From discovering new artists, to funding the artists' next project, to promoting new music to the larger public, and finding gigs, concerts, producers, studio time, and other supporting activities, a new model is taking shape in the music industry. Figure 3.3 shows this model and contrasts it to the more traditional, more vertically integrated model of the record company. Like TSMC's Open Innovation Platform from the previous chapter, a more open model is taking over from the traditional firms.

This crisis in the music industry is really the death knell of the traditional recording company business model, not the death of the music business itself. Music is perhaps more alive, more diverse, more engaged, and more connected to its audience than it has been in a half-century.

FIGURE 3.3   Digital Age Music Model

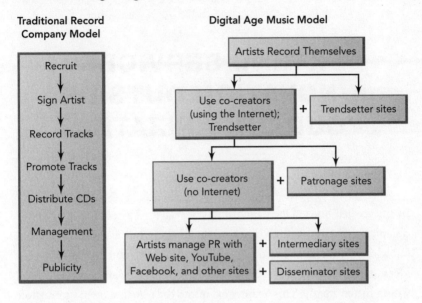

The business models that will succeed in the future music business will be those that help artists connect to their audiences, empower audiences to find artists they enjoy, capitalize on the enthusiasm of fans for certain artists, and spark co-creation between both groups.

o   o   o

Co-creation is a powerful innovative force across a wide variety of industries, from software to semiconductors to toys to music. It is also a way to create a deeper relationship with customers that will be harder for competitors to copy. It is a great way to escape from the commodity trap. Another avenue of escape is to become more open with both customers and many other participants in the environment surrounding your firm. That is the topic of the next chapter.

CHAPTER 4

EXTEND SERVICES INNOVATION OUTSIDE YOUR ORGANIZATION

In my earlier book, *Open Innovation,* I argued that companies should organize their innovation processes to become more open to external knowledge and ideas.[1] I also suggested that they let more of their internal ideas and knowledge flow to the outside when they were not being used within the company. This chapter examines the role that open innovation can play in services businesses as well.

Open innovation has a vitally important role in services in accessing external ideas and information for use in the services business and allowing unused ideas and information to be used outside in other services businesses. Open innovation in services requires us to leverage the power of specialization and the virtues of scope and scale. Deeper specialization enables open innovation to deliver economies of scope to the business, as well as economies of scale. It also enlists participation from many more individuals and companies than a company can accomplish on its own. This greater participation can lead to the creation and growth of business ecosystems that create and deliver more value for the business.

OPEN INNOVATION IN BRIEF

Open Innovation is a paradigm that assumes that firms can and should use external ideas as well as internal ideas, and internal and external paths to market, as they look to advance their business. Open Innovation combines internal and external ideas into new products, new architectures, and new systems. It also takes internal ideas to market through external channels, outside the current businesses of the firm, to generate additional value. Although it shares some important commonalities with open source software, there are also important differences.[2] The open innovation paradigm can be understood as the antithesis of a vertically integrated model of R&D. Open innovation is "the use of purposive inflows and outflows of knowledge to accelerate internal innovation, and expand the markets for external use of innovation, respectively."[3]

It can be helpful to visualize the vertically integrated model of R&D, and then compare it to the Open Innovation model. Figures 4.1 and 4.2 show this comparison. In Figure 4.1, projects move from a company's science and technology base to the market through internal R&D. This is a closed system because there is only one way into the process (at the outset, from the science and technology base of the firm) and only one way out of the process (via the market).

AT&T's Bell Laboratories stands as an exemplar of this model. It had many notable research achievements, but a notoriously inwardly focused culture. For example, AT&T pioneered the transistor, but it took ten years for the company to ship a product with a transistor in it.

FIGURE 4.1   The Closed Innovation Paradigm

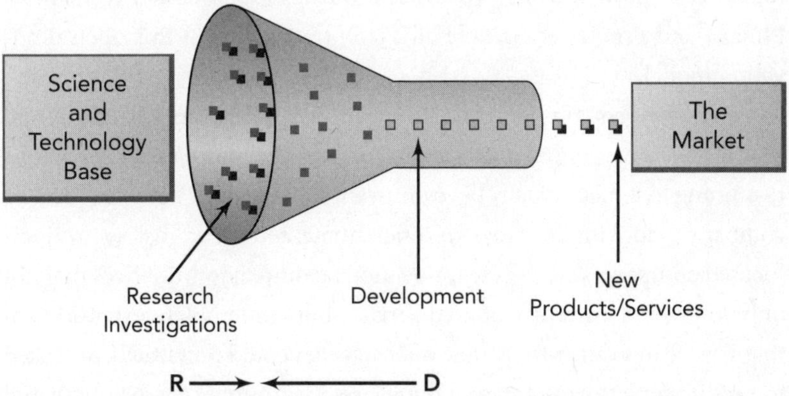

Research Investigations   Development   New Products/Services

R ⟶ ⟵ D

Source: © 2004 Henry Chesbrough.

69

FIGURE 4.2   The Open Innovation Paradigm

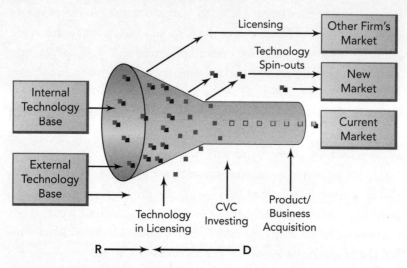

Source: © 2004 Henry Chesbrough.

Figure 4.2 shows a representation of an Open Innovation model. Here, projects can be launched from either internal or external technology sources, and new technology can enter into the R&D process at various stages. Projects go to market in many ways as well, through outlicensing or a spin-out venture company or through the company's own marketing and sales channels. This model is open because there are many ways for ideas to flow into the process and out into the market. IBM, Intel, Philips, and Procter & Gamble all exemplify aspects of this open innovation model.

Most services companies do not have formal R&D organizations, and few, if any, have funnel diagrams to manage their innovation processes (assuming that they actually have innovation processes). Yet every services company is looking for ways to differentiate and grow, just as product-focused companies are. These innovations require new initiatives that not only improve a currently offered service, but contemplate extensions of that service or even entirely new offerings that could potentially be linked to products, platforms, or something else. By grouping these growth and differentiation initiatives together, one can create a portfolio of projects

FIGURE 4.3   U.S. Industrial R&D by Firm Size

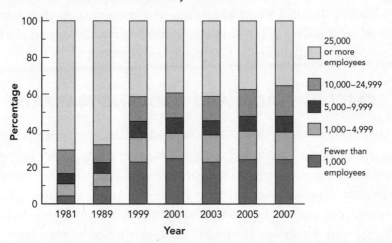

Source: National Science Foundation, Science Resource Studies, *Survey of Industrial Research Development* (1999, 2001, 2003, 2006, 2008).

that are every bit as innovative as those of product and technology companies.

More recent data have come out since *Open Innovation* was published in 2003 that continues to suggest a more level playing field for industrial innovation activity. U.S. data from the National Science Foundation (Figure 4.3) show that small firms (defined here as those with fewer than a thousand employees) continue to increase their share of the total amount of industrial R&D spending, amounting to almost 25 percent of total industry spending in 2007. Large firms (defined here as firms with more than twenty-five thousand employees) have seen their collective share of industrial R&D fall to 35 percent of total industry spending in that year. This is a marked decrease from the 1999 data I used in *Open Innovation*.

These data, and other data such as the growth of employment in small enterprises relative to employment in large firms, all combine to suggest that the playing field for innovation is becoming more level. Put differently, there are fewer economies of scale in R&D than there were a generation ago.[4] In a more distributed environment, where organizations of every size have potentially valuable technologies, firms of all sizes would do well to make extensive use of external technologies and ideas.

As smaller firms become collectively more important to innovation, it becomes clear that we are witnessing a greater degree of specialization in innovation activity. It is worth understanding specialization in more detail because it is the engine that powers open innovation.

SPECIALIZATION AND GROWING MARKETS

The economist George Stigler once observed that the extent of economic specialization was limited by the extent of the market.[5] As market activity expanded, more opportunities existed for economic actors to deepen their own expertise in one activity and trade for access to other items that were needed (instead of trying to obtain all the needed items themselves). To see this, think about the typical subsistence farmer of more than a hundred years ago. That farmer grew crops, raised chickens and pigs, perhaps grazed cattle and sheep, milked cows, and bartered time during the harvest with other farmers to bring in the crops. Most of the food that nineteenth-century farmers ate came from their own or nearby farms.

Today's modern farmers, by contrast, focus on one (or, at most, a very few) crop or specialize instead in raising chickens, or pigs, or cattle. They have access to highly specialized machinery, as well as the latest research on seed types, fertilizers, pesticides, watering systems, and the like. And when they take their crops or animals to market, the prices are set on national or international exchanges, complete with the option of forward contracts for many of the most common agricultural commodities. Today's farmers probably eat better than their nineteenth-century predecessors, but little, if any, of their food now comes from their own farms. As a result of this much more specialized system, the output of today's farmers dwarfs that of their predecessors and is the reason that less than 5 percent of the labor force can feed the entire population today in most advanced economies.

The causality in Stigler's observation might also run the other way, and perhaps firms can extend their markets by increasing their specialization. Such a phenomenon would provide firms with the ability to widen their markets by specialization that unleashes a virtuous cycle of economic growth. Specialization would create economic efficiencies, promoting an expanding market, that could encourage and reward further specialization, and so the cycle would repeat.

Another economist, Ronald Coase, observed that economic activity is conducted within firms when the costs of using the market to organize that activity are excessive. The many aspects of having the activity performed outside the firm he referred to as "transactions costs."[6] And whenever transactions costs were high (relative to their benefits), firms would conduct those activities inside their own four walls. But the costs and benefits of organizing an activity through the market are not fixed in stone; they can be influenced by the level of knowledge possessed within a firm, compared to the available knowledge for that activity that exists outside the firm. If sufficient knowledge and experience accumulate outside a firm for performing an activity, that activity may shift from being performed within the firm to one performed in the market.

Paychex: A Specialized Payroll Processor

An example of such shifting activity is payroll processing: the process of writing the checks each pay period (weekly, biweekly, or monthly) for a firm's workers. For centuries, firms handled the process for paying their own workers. It was not onerous to do so, and there was no alternative. Having someone else issue the paychecks to those workers would require transferring substantial amounts of knowledge about each worker's salary, any changes in that salary, all new employees to the firm, and any employee departures from the firm on a regular basis. As firms adopted vacation, sick leave, and tax-withholding policies in the twentieth century, there was a need to keep track of more accruals for each worker as well. In addition, the firm would have to trust that the outside payer would not run off with the money instead of paying it to its workers. These many transactions costs kept payroll processing organized within the firm.

Today a great many firms use external companies to process their payroll. The transactions costs noted above remain, but specialization has tipped the balance for many firms from doing it inside to sending it outside. Information technology plays an important supporting role here. The spread of computers has enabled firms to track copious amounts of data for employees reliably. Initially not all businesses could afford computers, so the haves (those that invested in the computers) had a technology advantage over the have-nots. And computers were not yet general-purpose systems, but were developed and programmed to perform fairly specific functions.[7]

The largest companies could justify purchasing computers for their own uses (initially accounting and control uses), but most others could not. The door was opened for firms that could justify a computer to support the payroll processing of multiple firms, each of them too small to pay for a computer. These advantages gave rise to firms like Paychex, which has built a significant business around the idea of providing payroll services to companies instead of those companies writing their own payroll checks.

This initial advantage for Paychex was one of economies of scale. By serving many companies, Paychex could afford the large fixed investment of a large computer system to do payroll. Its client companies, initially most of them smaller companies, could not afford to do this at that time, through the 1970s into the early 1980s.

With the passage of time, however, computing power became dramatically less expensive. This ought to have negated much or all of the scale advantage for outside providers like Paychex. However, these providers developed a second advantage that has supplanted their initial advantage, and this advantage has proven more enduring. This is the advantage of greater specialized knowledge, gained by far greater experience with processing payroll. By performing the function for many, many companies, providers like Paychex have developed tremendous expertise in this function—expertise beyond that possessed by any individual company meeting its own payroll.

Even something as seemingly simple as payroll processing can be complex. There are regulations at the national, state, and sometimes local levels to observe, with variations among all these regulations. There are international employees, and sometimes expatriate employees working overseas. There are evolving policies in withholding for tax purposes, as well as various benefit programs that the employee pays for and therefore are subtracted from his or her paycheck. These include 401k and 403bs plans, medical spending accounts, dental spending accounts, and so on.

Specialized providers who live with these complexities every day in the course of their business naturally become more adept in dealing with them at lower cost than most other firms, which wrestle with them intermittently, if they are even aware of them.

Specialized providers like Paychex also provide attractive career paths for employees who specialize in performing these tasks. Such people can achieve greater responsibility and compensation than they likely ever would achieve doing payroll work inside a typical firm.

So specialization alters the transactions costs of performing the process for the provider. If transactions costs change enough, the calculation of whether to "make" the process internally or "buy" that same process outside the firm can change as well. When buying becomes more attractive, open innovation becomes increasingly necessary. If firms can sufficiently specialize in performing an activity over time, they can become so efficient at performing that activity (relative to companies doing it themselves) that they can induce that activity to be performed outside potential customers' internal operations instead of within those operations. The overall market for that activity thus expands. This then enables the supplying firm to garner still more expertise and become even more efficient at the task, which leads to another round of shifting or level of activity, leading to market expansion. Firms in theory can enlarge their markets indefinitely by becoming highly specialized and highly skilled at specific economic activities.

Open innovation in services thus rests on a practical foundation: saving money for the customer while developing greater capability as a provider. Specialization by the provider promotes and deepens this foundation. When specialization joins co-creation, customers specialize as well and develop an even deeper relationship with their provider.

SERVICES AS A SET OF PROCESSES

The payroll processing example illustrates an important point: a business (whether a product or a service) can be conceived of as a series of processes that convert inputs into outputs through a series of specified activities or steps.

The field of industrial engineering is devoted to studying and improving many such processes. The origins of process engineering hearken back to the early twentieth century when Frederick Taylor studied men working on manual processes. Using a stopwatch and close observation, Taylor engineered improved methods for performing tasks with less wasted motion and greater efficiency.

Process engineering, which developed and matured in the manufacturing sector, is now coming to the services sector. Like any other process, it requires carefully observing and recording the activities necessary to transform the input into an output. Unlike manufacturing, many transformations of inputs into outputs in services take one piece of information as an input and create a new piece of information as an output. A simple example is processing a bank's loan application. The buyer's credit history information might be the input, and the approval decision of yes or no would be the output of the application review process.

Once processes are documented, they can be improved. While Taylor's stopwatch is unlikely to be of much help today, there are often unnecessary steps in a service process that can be eliminated or reordered so as to save time and money. In other cases, as in the earlier FedEx example, it may make more sense to let customers perform some of those steps directly as co-creators, as we discussed in Chapter Two. The improvement of these processes enables companies to revisit the make-or-buy decision for those processes.

To return to the point above, these services processes are developed and coordinated to create and deliver offerings to customers, receive payment for those offerings, and handle issues that might arise after the offerings are purchased. Once the processes to employ in the business are defined, it is a short step to deciding which to buy from outside and which to offer to others.

Consider some of the following services processes that firms must execute in the course of doing business:

- Paying suppliers
- Shipping goods and documents

- Acquiring and retaining customers
- Hiring and managing employees

Thirty years ago, each of these processes was largely conducted within each firm. Today there are specialized firms that offer services for each of them. Companies offering enterprise resource planning systems, such as SAP, incorporate modules to pay suppliers for the orders they send. UPS, among others, offers companies the opportunity to use UPS as their shipping department for all shipments through whatever means (even using the U.S. Postal Service). Salesforce.com allows companies to manage their customer relationships with their hosted software. And Peoplesoft (now owned by Oracle) helps companies hire and manage employees. The same gains from specialization that arose with payroll processing are accruing to these activities as well and across many firms in many different industries.

This begs the question: With all the potential processes provided by so many potential providers, how can a firm decide whether to retain any processes internally at all? Can it outsource all of its processes to others? Should it do so? The answer is that firms may in fact be able to outsource just about all of their processes (except perhaps those that organize the outsourcing of its constituent processes). But it would be unwise to do so. Not only are there the transactions costs that Ronald Coase and Oliver Williamson warn about. There is a deeper issue: the ability to develop certain processes that are truly differentiated from those of others. These genuinely superior processes can confer meaningful competitive advantage. Outsourcing these processes—let's call them "core processes"—would forfeit the ability to differentiate and sustain any competitive advantage over time. If one's processes are purchased from suppliers, those suppliers will sell those processes to other companies as well, thereby negating the ability to be different from all those others. And outsourcing this to others forfeits your chance to develop further specialization from the tacit knowledge you gain through providing the process directly. So even in a world of deep and wide specialization, firms ought to retain their core processes.[8] Nevertheless, in some instances, being more open with one's own core processes may boost additional growth opportunities, a point we return to below.

SPECIALIZATION AND ECONOMIES OF SCALE AND SCOPE

Economies of scale means doing one thing very well at very high volume. *Economies of scope* means doing lots of things under one roof. At first glance, economies of scale seem antithetical to economies of scope, and there is indeed tension between them. But a little reflection allows us to see more deeply into both types of economy. Both derive from greater specialization of capital and labor. I begin by defining the two terms more precisely and then explore their implications in the services context and open innovation. In the course of the exposition, the role that openness can play in advancing both sorts of economies will become clear.

Economies of Scale

The term *economies of scale* reflects the reduction of cost of some item as more volume of that item is produced. The intuition behind economies of scale becomes obvious in a manufacturing context. If manufacturing a particular item requires a large manufacturing plant, then the more units of that item that can be produced by that plant, the more the fixed costs of the plant (the land, the depreciation on the facility, the depreciation on the equipment used in the process, the plant manager's salary, and many others) can be spread over each item. By spreading these costs, the cost to produce each item is lower (the "economy" in *economies of scale*) as unit volumes increase. This continues until the plant cannot produce any further volume because its processes are running at maximum output or capacity, three shifts a day, seven days a week. At that point, further volume increases would require building another plant. Then the same calculation would start over with the new plant and its associated fixed costs.

Economies of scale contribute to services innovation at two levels. The first is that many of the assets needed to access, store, retrieve, and use the requisite information needed to supply a service require fixed investments. Information technology, in the form of computers, servers, routers, switches, and software, all share the property of the manufacturing plant above: their fixed costs of acquisition can be lowered if they are spread over more volume (here, more volume of services rather than more items produced). Whenever physical assets are employed in supplying services, their costs per transaction or per use are lower when those assets can be shared across more transactions or uses.

The second level in which economies of scale contribute to services innovation is perhaps more interesting. It comes from gains from increased knowledge accumulated through more transactions or uses. We saw this with the Walmart example of hurricanes, beer, and Pop-Tarts in Chapter Three. Instead of spreading fixed costs of a physical asset across more volume, this second level develops greater knowledge over more volume and leverages that knowledge through future volume in turn. When you buy a book on Amazon, Amazon also tells you what other books other people have purchased with the book that you are buying. Amazon knows this, and knows it better than anyone else, because it handles more online book purchase transactions than any other book reseller. And your purchase adds just a bit more information to Amazon's ever increasing database of transactions. Amazon increases its knowledge edge over its competitors even as you increase your knowledge of possible other books to buy.

This knowledge-based economy of scale has another important property. Unlike fixed assets, the use of knowledge does not consume the asset or diminish its use for other transactions; indeed, each use increases the knowledge advantage by a small amount. Economist Paul Romer has termed this "non-rivalrous knowledge."[9] In simple terms, it means that unlike a manufacturing plant that eventually runs out of capacity, knowledge advantages of scale can continue to accumulate indefinitely. This is a case where larger scale (having more knowledge) is definitely better.

Economies of scale create a powerful economic force driving open innovation in services. Extending your innovation activity outside your organization can boost economies of scale. The knowledge-based portion of economies of scale is a perhaps less well understood but even more sustainable driving force. But economies of scale require standardized processes. The next economic force encourages companies to provide greater variety to their customers.

Economies of Scope

Economies of scope are quite different from economies of scale, which spread fixed costs across many transactions. Economies of scope refer to the efficiencies that result from offering multiple items from a single source.[10] Economies of scope enable a firm to perform a wide variety of activities for its customers, and often with relatively little additional cost for doing so. To return to manufacturing for a moment, economies of scope arise when a plant can make many different kinds of products from the same facility and equipment. In the banking world, cross-selling additional services to clients—for example, a client with a checking account is offered a savings account, or someone with a savings account is offered a mortgage or a home equity loan—is an example of economies of scope.

Shifting to an example from another services context, department stores provide shoppers with a wide variety of goods to choose from, all under one roof. In comparison to the corner store or a boutique, department stores offer their customers the opportunity to buy a variety of items with just one visit. This is the idea of one-stop shopping. A grocer who adds services in his store, like a bank ATM or movie rental kiosk, is also extending one-stop shopping to customers for more kinds of purchases.

Economies of scope are of great importance because of the critical role that customers and users play in services activities, as we saw in Chapters Two and Three. When you have a relationship with a customer, ask how you can obtain more value from that relationship. A process that can accommodate a wide variety of customers' needs offers many economic benefits to those customers. Those benefits could be the ability to park only once in a shopping trip, pay for a variety of items with a single purchase, receive the desired items in a convenient way, or have all one's assets and liabilities reflected in a single monthly statement.

The economic force behind economies of scope is the need to reduce the total cost of a product or service to the customer. Customers have a variety of costs beyond the actual purchase price of an item: search costs to locate and select items, purchasing costs, receiving costs, and other costs after purchase (think of the after-sale maintenance and service for automobiles in Chapter One of this book). Services that employ economies of scope are reducing the total costs of their customers by reducing these other elements of cost that add to the initial purchase price of an item.

Reducing your customers' costs is a benefit for them, and it provides a business benefit to you: it provides you with more revenue from your existing customer relationships. This can make you more significant as a provider to your customers and make them more likely to stay with you over time. You will also learn more from your customers this way and perhaps find additional unmet needs or hidden costs that you are able to address. Extending beyond your own organization can enable you to provide a more complete services offering to your customers. So this becomes the second powerful economic force underlying open innovation in services.

Building Service Platforms from Economies of Scope

Services innovation can help companies erect service platforms, which attract customers, and, most important, often a variety of other contributors, partners, resellers, and commentators as well. A recognizable example of a successful platform is iTunes by Apple, created for the iPod originally, on top of which multiple services have been developed. Initially iTunes was created to offer a wide variety of music for listeners. Whenever an old group wanted to offer a digital version of an old song, the group wanted to be sure that it was available on iTunes because of its reach to listeners. This in turn made iTunes increasingly able to supply more kinds of music to its customers from its site, making it the first place customers looked when they wished to purchase new music. Now iTunes is promoting TV and movies, games, books, and other items as well thanks to the broad appeal it has established as a platform.

iTunes has played a critical role in Apple's successful expansion of its iPod business as it entered into iPhones and iPads. With the iPhone, the Apple App Store Web site is attracting the most third-party cell phone software applications, again making it highly desirable for new applications to be offered there.[11] With the advent of the iPad, Apple is now leveraging the Apps Web site to support this device as well, so that the platform appeal automatically embraces it. It is small wonder that the iPad sold more than 3 million units in its first three months.[12] Meanwhile, the imitative tablet products coming out of Taiwan are trying to catch up. But like Motorola in Chapter One, these companies are trying to develop a better device, while Apple has developed an entire ecosystem with its device, its Apps, and all the third-party contributors to the platform. The imitators will need to develop their own platform or partner with companies like Google, RIM, or Microsoft, and differentiate it from that of Apple before they will have any chance of unseating Apple from its market-leading position. To create these ecosystems, companies must reach well beyond their own organization. In this instance, they must hope that they are not too late to the party and have aligned themselves with one of the winning platforms.

OPEN INNOVATION AND SPECIALIZATION

Specialization is an important consideration for innovation and the ability to grow. And it has quite a lot to do with openness. Firms can use openness as a means to gain greater economies of scale, economies of scope, or both. And I will argue in this section that some firms are managing to pursue both kinds of economy by following more open approaches to their business.

Openness generally refers to ways of sharing with others and inviting their participation. Scholars have studied the ways in which being open can elicit greater innovation in a variety of fields, from law to science to software to culture.[13] Here we examine a more specific form of openness—that defined in my earlier work on innovation in *Open Innovation* and *Open Business Models*. In these books, openness is not merely a good thing for society; it is also a new way to stimulate greater profitability for innovating companies.[14]

In the open innovation model, there are two complementary kinds of openness. One is outside in, where a company makes greater use of external ideas and technologies in its own business. Openness in this context means overcoming the not-invented-here syndrome and welcoming new external contributions much as the firm would welcome its own contributions.

The other kind of openness is inside out, in which a firm allows some of its own ideas and technologies to be used by others in its businesses. Openness here means overcoming the not-sold-here syndrome, in which the company prohibits any use of its ideas and technologies outside its own business. Revenues from external use of a company's ideas are as welcome as revenues from the company's own use of its ideas.

Let's consider each kind in turn.

Leveraging Outside-In Openness for Economies of Scope

Outside-in openness starts with the realization that as good as you are and as capable as you may be, there are a great many other smart, capable people who do not work for you. Initially this may seem to be a disappointing limitation, since it implies that you cannot corner the market on useful knowledge in a particular field.[15] But once you get over that fact, you may realize that this same reality confers some truly exciting opportunities as well. If there are lots of smart people in the world, consider what you can do to get some of them working with you.

In a services context, outside-in knowledge allows a company to provide additional elements to a service offer beyond the company's own knowledge and experience. Such additional elements extend the offer and provide more value and one-stop shopping for customers. As noted, customers have many costs beyond the actual purchase price for an item, and outside-in knowledge may help the service provider reduce the customer's total costs, which will allow that provider to satisfy their needs better, retain them longer, and so on.

A short example here will help make this concrete. (We explore numerous examples of this openness in Part Two.) Amazon is well known as the world's leading online seller of books. But Amazon also provides a great many other kinds of products on its Web site. Many of these other products, including some books, are not stocked by Amazon but are instead supplied by third-party merchants that post their products on Amazon's Web site. This is an instance of Amazon employing outside-in openness. Instead of stocking all of the products itself, the company provides a platform for other merchants to showcase their wares on Amazon's Web site. They literally provide these outside merchants with the same software interfaces that they use internally to generate the Web pages on the Amazon site. This software is one of Amazon's specializations that differentiate it from other online retailers. The third-party merchant pages on the Amazon Web site look just like the internal pages that Amazon uses for its own products. Usually customers can't discern any difference.[16]

Notice what this openness does for Amazon. It makes Amazon's site more attractive to more visitors. It allows customers who know Amazon's site, and its purchase process, to employ it for other purchases they would like to make beyond books. This not only makes Amazon more attractive as a site for online book purchases. It makes Amazon a leading shopping destination site on the Web for items of all kinds. It thus becomes an Internet shopping platform, which is a much larger opportunity for Amazon. Amazon records every transaction, building a still larger database of activity for its customers and the products they buy. This information helps Amazon accumulate more knowledge sooner across more kinds of purchases as a result of its outside-in openness.

Exploiting Inside-Out Openness for Economies of Scale

Openness can also stimulate greater economies of scale, but this is not outside-in openness discussed immediately above; it is inside-out openness that leads to further economies of scale.

A company should not outsource its core processes and have them supplied by other firms on behalf of it. But the reverse condition (that the company ought not to let others insource its core processes) may not be true. Sometimes a core process for the company might become even more efficient and effective if that process were offered for other firms to use as well.

This logic is not apparent to most executives I have encountered. They have a strong desire to restrict the access of a core process to their own business. In economic terms, this is treating the process as a monopsony, that is, a single buyer. The firm will "buy" the core process for its own use but refuse to let any other companies access that same process.

These core processes are those that truly differentiate the firm from its competitors. It is only natural, perhaps, that the business would not wish to share that differentiation with their competitors. But it is a big world out there, and many kinds of companies might actually benefit from using your core process—and use it in ways you never would. There are even situations where you would willingly let your core processes be used by competitors as long as they do so on your terms.

One example of a competitive firm that nonetheless frequently shares its core processes with other companies is Procter & Gamble (P&G). Historically it treated its core processes as highly restricted assets, but in recent years it has opened up access to those assets. One of their executives, Jeff Weedman, vice president of external business development, has developed a far more nuanced view of competitive advantage. "There are many kinds of competitive advantage," he says. "The original view was: I have got it, and you don't. Then there is the view, that I have got it, you have got it, but I have it cheaper. Then there is I have got it, you have got it, but I got it first. Then there is I have got it, you have got it from me, so I make money when I sell it, and I make money when you sell it."[17] This last form of competitive advantage is what can result from inside-out openness. As Steve Baggett, director of external business development at P&G, commented, "If you don't license, chances are very good that someone else has a very good technology too. It's rare that you're the only game in town. So do you want to participate in the licensing revenues or not?"

Indeed, P&G welcomes the notion of having its competitors use its technology. This is because competitors that employ P&G concepts are not striving for newer or even better concepts in their own labs. They become "happy followers" instead of "threatening leaders." Happy followers allow P&G to sustain industry leadership and help defray its costs of doing so because their payments cover some of the costs of developing the technology. That spreads the fixed costs of development over more volume, and that is what economies of scale are all about.

But the benefits of inside-out openness go even further. Sharing core processes with other firms increases the volume of activity that passes through those processes. With greater utilization and greater volume, these processes become further refined and advanced. This spreads the costs of developing the processes out over more volume, reducing their cost to P&G. It also gives P&G more exposure to more uses of its processes and the chance to learn more about their applicability from other businesses. All of this results in a greater accumulation of knowledge. This is the way to keep well ahead of the happy followers and keep them coming back to P&G for more in the future.

To assess whether this is a good deal for the happy followers requires considering their alternatives. If they have the global scale to achieve similar volumes for core processes that P&G has, then their best alternative is probably not to rely on P&G's processes but to develop their own instead (though they may want to emulate P&G's openness and share those processes with others for the right price). So expect a company like Unilever to employ its own core processes rather than use those of P&G.

But for every Unilever, there are dozens or hundreds of smaller consumer products companies that cannot hope to obtain the scale that P&G has. These smaller companies may be better off if they are able to access world-class processes (albeit for a price) from a P&G than they would be to incur the costs and risks of developing their own. These smaller companies will have to find other ways to differentiate themselves.

OPEN INNOVATION AND SERVICES INNOVATION

Like innovation in products and technologies, innovation in services benefits greatly from specialization. Even when intangible inputs are used to create intangible outputs, companies can develop greater skill and effectiveness by focusing on more specialized knowledge creation. With the embrace of outside-in open innovation, companies can provide greater economies of scope to their services customers. And with the use of inside-out open innovation, they can leverage their own core processes to establish powerful economies of scale in services, including the knowledge-based economies of scale that can extend indefinitely. Note that specialization works better when the company works with others outside its own organization. Opening services innovation is critical to establishing a winning edge through specialization.

Armed with the forces of scale and scope economies, services firms can get more value and more growth from their core capabilities. The highest and best use of these capabilities, though, is in open innovation approaches to construct business platforms. These platforms induce others to invest their time, money, energy, and ideas in extending your initiatives. As they do so, your platform becomes more attractive to more customers, while becoming more profitable and sustainable for you.

o   o   o

So far in this book, we have considered the special aspects of services innovation, their history, how they transform value chains of firms, the role of customers, and the role that openness plays in advancing both economies of scale and scope for innovating services firms. With this foundation, we are ready to examine the need to change the business model in order to become an effective Open Services innovator. That is the subject of the next chapter.

CHAPTER 5

TRANSFORM YOUR BUSINESS MODEL WITH SERVICES

While openness can be quite helpful itself to improve services innovation, it becomes far more powerful when joined to the task of designing or redesigning a business model. As we have already seen in this book, services innovation can transform your business model. Offering your product as a service can, for example, convert fixed costs for your customers into variable costs. Services innovation can help you stream-line your customers' processes, as when UPS took over its customers' shipping departments or Paychex took over payroll processing for its customers.

Services innovation in fact changes your business model in many ways. The distribution channels may change, and your interactions with customers will certainly change. The value chains may be affected as well, as in the situation we will see in the next chapter, where GE charges for its engines by the hour, locking in the aftermarket service for its engines. Gross margins are often lower for services than for products. Cash requirements also change as lumpy product revenues are replaced with smaller, smoother revenue streams from services.

In this chapter, we look more deeply into business models. We examine their importance and the difficulty companies have in innovating new models. We conclude with ways to organize to innovate new services business models and how to nurture and cultivate a services platform that attracts others to invest with and alongside your business.

DEFINING THE BUSINESS MODEL

A business model is a way to create value for a business and then to capture at least some of that value for the organization. More specifically, in my work with my colleague Richard Rosenbloom, we claimed that the business model fulfills the following functions:[1]

1. Articulating the value proposition, that is, the value created for users by the offering.

2. Identifying a market segment—the users to whom the offering is useful and for what purpose.

3. Defining the structure of the value chain that the firm requires to create and distribute the offering, and determine the complementary assets needed to support its position in this chain. This includes the firm's suppliers and customers and should extend from raw materials (or inputs) to the final customer.

4. Specifying the revenue generation mechanisms for the firm and estimating the cost structure and profit potential of producing the offering, given the value proposition and value chain structure chosen (profit and loss, and forecast).

5. Describing the position of the firm within the value network (also referred to as an ecosystem) linking suppliers and customers, including identification of potential complementers and competitors.

6. Formulating the competitive strategy by which the innovating firm will gain and hold advantage over rivals.

Although this definition was introduced for business models in the context of products and technologies, we explore its use in services.

BUSINESS MODELS FOR SERVICES INNOVATION

Services innovation can be focused on each of the attributes in the definition of the business model. We have already seen numerous examples of how a services focus can alter the value proposition for a business.

One way is by converting a fixed asset into a smaller variable expense that goes up and down with the business. Think of purchasing a car (the fixed asset) in comparison to purchasing transportation services (whether a taxi, a rental car, or a Zipcar). Variable expenses are often attractive to customers because they can avoid the high expense of a fixed asset. When business is good, the customer uses more of the service and can afford to pay more for it. And when business softens, the customer has the ability to use less of the service and owe less for it. This creates the value proposition of flexibility for the customer, along with the associated benefit of reduced initial capital outlays. This is sometimes termed a more asset-efficient way for the customer to do business. Often the customer can obtain a higher return on investment through this approach.

Once the services provider has invested in the fixed asset in order to provide the services, it can recover the investment in a number of ways:

- Leveraging the utilization advantage that allows the provider to obtain more value out of the fixed investment. If the provider is able to use the asset much more intensively, the fixed costs are spread over many more uses than any individual customer could. We saw this example in Chapter Two with transportation services.
- Redesigning the product and service to create new offers. Often this can be done by co-creating with customers to provide a service more closely tailored to customers' needs. We saw this in Chapter Three in Lego's offerings for adults and the rise of the vertically disintegrated digital music model.
- Exploiting the greater information gleaned from supporting lots of customers. Aggregating this information gives the provider a knowledge advantage that helps in improving and optimizing the asset and learning more about customers' needs. We saw this example in Chapter Four with Amazon.
- Opening up new markets for using the asset. These new markets might value the use of the asset at an equal or higher level than the initial market did. This is another advantage of openness for Amazon, discussed in Chapter Four.

The key element is that the provider of the services achieves a higher return on assets due to increased utilization of the service or asset beyond what the customer could have used for herself or himself. This creates a mutually beneficial relationship for the two parties.

Another way to redesign a business model is to change the target customer for the service. In health care, for example, the advance of technology is enabling meters that provide more accurate measures of the body's functions, such as blood glucose meters. With more accurate readings of blood sugars, diabetes services can now target the individual patient rather than the prescribing physician, who was the traditional customer.[2] In financial services, many companies now market their offerings directly to customers instead of using a network of brokers and advisors to promote their products. Changing the target customer requires making many changes in the business model in order to be effective.

A third method to innovate a business model is to redesign a value chain that creates and delivers the service in a more effective way. Using economies of scope, you can offer to take over one of the customer's processes. This embeds you inside the customer, lets you see more of the entire picture of how the service is consumed, and helps you create improvements that reduce your costs of providing the service further. (We will see this with Xerox in printers in Chapter Six, and Alstom in the London Tube in Chapter Ten.) As we will see with GE in aircraft engines in Chapter Six, this generated an advantageous position versus aftermarket rivals for the maintenance, service, and support of engines already installed.

A fourth way to shift your business model is to change the way that you charge for it, which often shifts other elements of the model, such as the value proposition. Some services now are provided free but subject the customer to advertising in return, which many customers find to be an attractive value proposition. This has been a difficult challenge for newspapers in comparison to online news services. Airlines like Ryanair have unbundled the various services they provide during a flight, such as check-in at the ticket counter, the baggage checked on the flight, drinks, food, and most recently proposed, even the use of the toilet on the aircraft.[3] This unbundling allows Ryanair to charge very low ticket prices for its flights and get more money from its passengers from the now-unbundled ancillary services. Unsuspecting customers, however, will find that by the time they have checked a bag, purchased some food and drink, used the lavatory, and so forth, their bargain-priced ticket will seem more expensive than they might have anticipated.

A final way to innovate a business model is to link into a larger business network or ecosystem or, ideally, create one of your own. Connecting to a larger network raises your profile within that network and brings others using that network to you as a possible provider. The network also helps you specialize your services by allowing you to team up with complementary providers of other services instead of supplying them yourself. If you can create your own, you have the possibility of building a platform for your service. This can attract other providers to your network and give customers an assortment of choices, without requiring you to invest in the provision of those choices.

Coordinating the Various Activities in Business Models

Business models involve a dynamic and complex set of activities. As companies grow and their staff expands, it becomes more challenging to keep everything and everyone pointed in the same direction. When the many activities of a business are properly aligned, the business performs better than when some of the activities are working at cross-purposes.

One of the ways in which companies are able to align their people and activities with the direction they wish to head in is through a dominant logic of the business: a set of heuristic rules, norms, and beliefs that managers create to guide their actions.[4] Xerox historically made most of its money from its copiers, printers, and the toner supplying them. Anything that made more copies faster was good for the business. This logic usefully focuses managers' attention as they seek new opportunities for the firm. It facilitates organizational coordination across different parts of the company and brings coherence to the many disparate activities of the company, helping to improve its performance and reduce wasteful or inappropriate endeavors.

Also important are the things that a dominant logic implicitly filters out: the ideas and behaviors that do not fit with the dominant logic. Xerox's dominant logic caused it to neglect the small business and home office market, since these customers used copiers and printers more sporadically than larger firms did. This filtering process works to maintain focus and internal coherence among the firm's activities. It stops firms from starting distracting initiatives and discourages further investment in initiatives that somehow got started but clearly do not belong in the firm.

This is where the business model comes in. It provides a coherent framework that takes product or service or technology characteristics and potentials as inputs and converts them through customers and markets into economic outputs. The business model is a key link in the process of economic value creation within any firm. When a model has been highly successful, it becomes part of the dominant logic of that firm.

Dell's direct-to-consumer business model became part of how it developed and differentiated itself in its market. This model helped Dell grow from a college dorm room start-up to one of the largest computer companies in the world. Although the logic of that model was subtle and pervasive, it affected everything from supplier relations to engineering design to shipping and credit. Competitors struggled for many years to imitate the model. Because it worked as a system, simply copying one or two of its features did not deliver the same results. So a successful business model also became a source of competitive advantage for Dell. It prospered by developing a business model logic of selling its products directly to its customers instead of relying on retailers or resellers.

The Inertia of a Successful Business Model

Coherence among the many parts of one's business is quite valuable. In business, managers often have to confront ambiguous situations where the best choice is not immediately clear. A coherent business model helps managers in these situations understand how to think about new information, what to focus on, and what to leave alone. Although this business model logic is useful and beneficial, it comes at a cost. The choice of business model constrains other choices, filtering out certain possibilities, even as other prospects are logically reinforced.[5] The logic of a business model can become a source of inertia, and a very successful business model can become a powerful source of inertia.

Recent history provides many examples of this inertia, why it is strong, and why it is often hard to overcome. During the dot-com boom, many businesses were wondering whether and how to do business on the Internet.[6] There were a number of conflicting viewpoints. One was the perspective of distributing mainly through bricks-and-mortar channels. They regarded the use of a company's own Web site for direct sale of its products as direct competition with their own storefronts. The company's own sales executives, who had quarterly and annual sales quotas through these channels, were powerful and determined advocates for the storefronts and strongly resisted any effort to have the company sell its products directly through the Internet. They wanted this business for the storefronts. These conflicts created a powerful source of inertia that held back the move to online business for many companies during this period.[7]

Dell itself has had to deal with the powerful inertia of its direct-to-consumer business model. In recent years, the company has introduced new types of products to the market that have not succeeded. One failed new product was the Dell DJ, Dell's response to the iPod from Apple. But as a new kind of product, Dell customers needed to see and touch and feel the DJ before they were willing to buy it. There was no easy way for Dell to do this, since it sold all of its products directly to the customer. The DJ never took off, and Dell pulled it from the market.

Being able to look at, hold, play with, and experiment with products before purchasing them is one of the lasting benefits of retail storefronts. They provide potential customers with the chance to encounter a new product before having to purchase it. Apple's retail stores have been phenomenally successful. Some analysts claim that these stores generate higher revenue per square foot than any other retail store in the United States.[8] And Apple has been quite effective in introducing new kinds of products to customers.

In the online, direct-to-consumer world, it is very efficient to buy when you already know what it is that you want. But the direct business model is limiting in its ability to introduce a new kind of product to consumers. Dell has slowly begun to introduce itself into selected retail storefronts again. But this is a different kind of business, so Dell has had to proceed slowly, since it knows that its dominant logic works against the use of retail distribution for its products.

TOOLS TO TRANSFORM YOUR BUSINESS MODEL

Business models are valuable, but over time successful models develop inertia and become hard to change. When business models are no longer effective, they have to be changed, and this inertia must be overcome. An alternative business model must be developed in order to restore growth and profitability to the business.

One promising approach for developing alternatives is to construct maps of business model activities that clarify their underlying processes. Once this is done, these underlying processes can then be recombined into possible new models. This often requires a series of experiments as different combinations of processes are considered and some tested. One example of this mapping approach comes from Alex Osterwalder, a business model design consultant who also created a nine-point decomposition that characterizes a business model (see Figure 5.1).

Osterwalder advises organizations to use this design as a tool to describe their current business model and envision alternatives. Other ways to use this type of tool include mapping out a competitor's business model and comparing that map to your own. Differences between the models might suggest ways to further differentiate from your competitor or perhaps ways to imitate a successful competitor.

Another way to use this map is to outline some successful business models from other industries and compare those to your own model. Again, the comparison might suggest ways to emulate some aspect of a successful model from outside your industry (assuming that you judge that it is likely to work well in your industry).

FIGURE 5.1   Osterwalder's Depiction of a Business Model

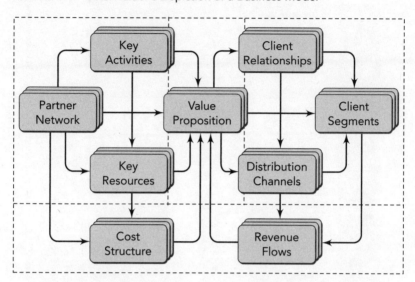

Source: A. Osterwalder, *Business Model Generation* (Hoboken, N.J.: Wiley, 2009), p. 44.

Still another effective way to employ this approach is to look outside your own business to the companies around you. It can be helpful to map a key customer's business model, in the business-to-business context, so that you can pitch an offering that aligns more closely with the customer's revenue and profit engine. The same analysis is helpful in understanding key suppliers and whether their business model is aligned with your own model or is fundamentally in conflict. Finally, these maps can help you select potential alliance partners from a group of prospective firms. Since firms' models differ, alliances with firms whose business models are most compatible with your own are a good way to build more enduring alliances.

There are other mapping tools as well. One approach comes from the concept of component business modeling, which provides a greater amount of detail in the business model. IBM has been an early leader in this area and has published white papers on the approach and filed patents on the method. The greater detail is quite helpful in developing your own business model further. It can be hard to collect enough detail from other companies to develop comparison maps for them (unless you have some consultants working with you to fill in those details). Figure 5.2 shows a visual depiction of IBM's view of a component business model.

FIGURE 5.2 IBM's Depiction of a Component Business Model

	Business Administration	New Business Development	Relationship Management	Servicing and Sales	Product Fulfilment	Financial Contol and Accounting
Direct	Business Planning	Sector Planning	Account Planning	Sales Planning	Fulfilment Planning	Portfolio Planning
Control	Business Unit Tracking Staff Appraisals	Sector Management Product Management	Relationship Management Credit Assessment	Sales Management	Fulfilment Planning	Compliance Reconciliation
Execute	Staff Administration Product Administration	Product Delivery Marketing Campaigns	Credit Administration	Sales Customer Dialogue Contact Routing	Product Fulfilment Document Management	Customer Accounts General Ledger

Source: IBM Global Business Services, "The Component Business Model," n.d., https://www-935.ibm.com/services/us/iimc/pdf/g510-6163-component-business-models.pdf.

These modeling approaches provide a way to experiment with alternative business models by enabling firms to articulate their own business model and then simulate various possible models they might adopt. They also have the great virtue of explicitly showing the processes underlying a business model, so that people in one part of the organization see their role and how it influences others in different parts of the organization. Thus, the earlier descriptions of configuring elements of a business model now can become far more concrete.

These maps can expose the underlying activities in your current business model. They can also identify areas where the activities are mutually supportive (or coherent), or perhaps where they are inconsistent. If Ryanair wants to sell more beverages during its flights, for example, is it logically consistent to charge for the use of toilets in the aircraft? Whatever the case, knowing how to describe your business model and its underlying activities is a prerequisite for innovating and improving its effectiveness.

From Maps to Alternative Business Models

Tools such as mapping are useful to explicate business models, but by themselves they do nothing to promote experimentation and innovation with those models. For that, you will need organizational processes and authority to undertake the experiments, and then the ability to take actions based on results from those tests.

One set of processes relates to experimentation. My colleague Stefan Thomke at Harvard Business School has developed some excellent ideas on how to do good experiments in business.[9] One concept is the fidelity of the experiment: the extent to which the experimental conditions are representative of the larger market. Real economic transactions, involving real customers who pay real money under an alternative business model, provide the highest fidelity. Another concept is the cost of conducting the test. A third issue is the time required to obtain feedback from the experiment. Also important is the amount of information learned from the test.

To manage experiments effectively and learn from them, separating a failed outcome from a mistake is critical. The former is quite useful, and a natural outcome of the experimentation process. Every successful result is preceded by numerous failed outcomes along the way. Understanding why the experiment failed and how to adjust the experiment to increase its chance of success is the way organizations learn.

Mistakes are quite different in character. An experiment that is poorly designed so that nothing new is learned from the experiment is a mistake. Repeating an experiment that failed before without changing the conditions of the experiment (and therefore failing again) is a mistake. In contrast to failures, mistakes teach us nothing, so they waste time, resources, and initiative.

Companies should strive to develop processes that provide high fidelity at low cost, in a short period of time, with expectations of cumulative learning from a series of failures, before discovering a viable alternative business model. Companies need a culture that supports failure as a healthy and necessary part of innovation and reserves its condemnation for mistakes.

A Bias for Action

Beyond designing experiments is the need for firms to have a bias for action. This is particularly appropriate in situations of rapid change, where the right business model is far from obvious and a perfect one may not be achievable given time constraints. In these situations, there is a paucity of data with which to make decisions. Therefore, the data will have to be created before they can be analyzed. Entrepreneurs who create new businesses and associated business models do not analyze their environment so much as they take actions that create new information that reveals latent possibilities in that environment. In other words, they do not study the market as much as they enact it.[10] Absent action, no additional data will be forthcoming.

This is one of the key advantages of start-up companies. They have no legacy business model to protect and defend, no dominant logic inherited from a successful business model to overcome. They can try something, watch the response, adapt to that response, and try something else. Larger companies typically cannot make decisions as quickly as these small companies can. So while start-ups lack many of the resources of the larger companies, they have an evolutionary advantage in their ability to adapt more quickly. As Darwin advised us, "It is not the strongest of the species that survives, nor the most intelligent that survives. It is the one that is the most adaptable to change."

It is unlikely that larger companies will be able to move as quickly as these smaller organizations are able to do. A good way to deal with that reality is to pay close attention to the experiments that these start-up firms in your industry represent. Chances are that these new entrants in your industry are trying to compete with a different business model. This is especially true if they have been able to raise outside capital investment as part of their entry. Happily, most start-up companies are eager to talk with larger companies in their industry. They are seeking partnerships, alliances, possible customers, and third-party validation of their companies. By meeting with them and learning about their business model, you might stimulate some creative thinking in your organization about how you might revisit your own business model.

Leading the Business Model Change

This brings us to a third process that is vital for changing the business models of already existing organizations: leading change in an organization. Leading the change process for new business models is not an easy task. Business models develop strong coherence and strong inertia, making them hard to change. This problem is compounded by the fact that it is not always clear who within an organization has the responsibility and authority to manage this process. Functional heads do not have authority over the whole organization, and business models require changing aspects of and interactions among operations, engineering, marketing, sales, and finance. There may well be conflicts among some or all of these functions in business model innovation.

CEOs of small companies may be ideally suited to the task, especially if they are owners of the business as well. But the CEOs of larger firms must rely on middle managers, particularly if the businesses within the company are diverse. Too much of the important information in each business resides in these middle managers, and the CEO isn't close enough to each business to know how best to improve each business model. A further problem stems from relying on the CEO: he or she rose to the position under the current business model. That model is deeply familiar, even comforting, to the CEO, and potential alternative models can be unfamiliar and even threatening to him or her. In these circumstances, the CEO may actually retard the innovation process rather than lead it.

Outside investors are another source of possible inertia. The current business model is part of the investment story that prompted investors to buy shares in the company. Changing the business model might alter that story, and it may not be obvious at the outset whether a new model is going to perform better than the current one.

Another possible locus of business model innovation could be the general managers of the specific businesses in a company with multiple units. These managers in larger firms may have the authority to change their business model, but typically they are rotated from one position to another every two or three years. This may be too little time to formulate the experiments, conduct them, collect and analyze the data, develop inferences and interpretations of those data, and then reframe the analysis in ways that are sufficiently persuasive to guide the transformation to a new business model. Instead, these general managers may content themselves to do the best they can with the business model they've got. After all, the risks of developing a new model might materialize during their tenure, and many of the benefits of a new model might become apparent only during a successor's tenure as the manager of that business.

Clearly, finding the necessary leadership to innovate business models in services can be a challenge.

REORGANIZING FOR A SERVICES BUSINESS MODEL

Along with innovating the business model design is the need to think through how to structure the organization to implement a new services business model. In most product organizations, the services function is treated as a support function: something that must be provided but not something that makes the difference between success and failure in the market.

In services-oriented firms, the situation is quite different. The services function is recognized as being vital to competitive success in the market. Services are a primary source of revenue, provide close links to customers, and keep customers satisfied so that they don't switch their business to competitors. With the leverage provided by focus and specialization, these services become highly profitable over time.

Such critical business functions are managed by highly capable people, whose careers can readily extend to the most senior levels of the firm. Services executives are regarded as key assets in the organization.

Setting Up the Organization for Economies of Scale and Scope

An organization striving for economies of scale will optimize the way it does a few things very, very well and becomes highly capable of accomplishing those selected tasks. But it is less able to shift to other tasks, precisely because it is optimized for its chosen few.

An organization striving for economies of scope will work very hard to give customers as much of what they want as it can. It will also assume that the customer may want some new activity or service provided in the future. Such organizations have to be flexible at doing a number of things rather than specialized at mastering a select few.

Some leading companies are pioneering new organizational structures that better manage the tensions between customized service solutions for customers and achieving economic efficiency in delivering those services. To simplify these structures considerably, these companies have split themselves into customer-facing front-end units linked to standardized back-end processes. The front-end customer-facing units develop, package, and deliver customized solutions for individual clients. They generate revenues and profits, with the organizational clout to match, and focus on satisfying the customer.

Some large companies that have developed growing services business models—in addition to IBM, these include Sun Microsystems,

ABB, Nokia, and Ericsson—have adopted the front-end and back-end approaches to put more focus on services in their businesses while maintaining economic efficiencies.[11] IBM's current CEO comes from the organization that focused on the customer at IBM: its Global Services business unit. Such customer-facing units have power and the ability to search across the organization for the best solutions to customers' needs.

The back-end function of these new organizations provides standardized services that can easily be reconfigured at little or no cost for individual customers. The idea is for back-end units to provide reusable elements that can be mixed and matched in different combinations by the front-end units. These back-end units thus focus on minimizing costs through high utilization of assets and frequent reuse of standardized processes from one customer to another.[12] These units also have real power. Any reasonably large organization will be unable to serve its customers' needs if it cannot do so efficiently. As we saw with Taiwan Semiconductor Manufacturing Corporation (TSMC) in Chapter Four, service providers can impose certain restrictions on their clients, precisely so that they can fulfill their needs for a variety of items effectively and efficiently. This ability to scale with volume while supporting flexibility requires a careful balancing of variety with process restrictions that tie customers to TSMC's design and manufacturing tools or tools from third parties that TSMC certifies.

Ericsson estimates that up to 75 percent of the services component of its solutions can be based on off-the-shelf reusable components. The remaining services must be customized by the front-end unit at the point of contact with the customer. The combination of one-stop shopping on the front end that faces the customer, combined with reconfigurable resources on the back end that process the transactions, can simultaneously achieve better economies of scope and economies of scale relative to the traditional product organization.[13]

Organizing the back end includes being able and willing to use processes that can handle the highest volumes of transactions. Only a small number of organizations receive enough activity to sustain these best-in-class processes at a very large scale. Most others need to partner with an organization that provides such capabilities—one kind of openness explored in the previous chapter. Alternatively, the few organizations able to attain best-in-class processes will need to offer their back end to other organizations in order to attract enough volume to reach this scale of transactions, generating another kind of openness that we discussed in the previous chapter.

Nurturing the Platform for Your Business Model

Getting your own organizational structure realigned is only part of what is needed to take advantage of services. The ultimate goal for a services business is to become a platform for other businesses to build on. This requires opening up your organization's business model to harness the energy and investment of third parties in the business.

In my previous book, *Open Business Models,* I developed a hierarchical typology of business models. At the bottom of this typology was the commodity business model.[14] This model requires little investment to start, but provides no differentiation and therefore little long-term value. At the top of the hierarchy was the most valuable type of business model: the platform business model. This model requires extensive investment and development but provides tremendous differentiation and long-term value for the firm. The crowning achievement of a platform business model is that it attracts external companies to invest in business activities that enhance the value of your platform. Stated differently, a platform business model leverages other people's money and resources as it grows.

A successful platform can be thought of as a two-sided market between suppliers and customers. On one side of the market is a wealth of suppliers providing numerous choices for customers to choose from. On the other side are lots of customers looking for items to choose. The more choices there are, the more customers come, and the more customers who come, the more choices are offered. A virtuous cycle between the supply and demand side of the market results from this happy confluence. This does not arise by accident; it results from a conscious policy to involve others in one's own offerings. Then the platform developer must create an architecture to connect the internal and external elements.

This has been the happy achievement for Apple's iPod, iTunes, iPhone, and iPad. These hardware devices and online services together constitute a powerful platform business model. On the supply side of the market, the success of these offerings now elicits new types of investment by both new entrants to the market and established firms, which add to the value of the platform. Some of these investments create new accessories, services, and products for the devices, to be delivered through or on the platform. Others create new applications and services that can run on the devices, as well as accessory products. Still other suppliers or developers adapt these devices to new uses and enable them to be used in new markets (one example, iPod Touch, has evolved into a powerful gaming platform that competes with Nintendo's Wii, among other game players).

The embrace of your platform by others can create a virtuous cycle that reinforces your value and induces even more entrants to join. When new music acts cut new tracks, they want to get those on iTunes first, since it has the lion's share of the digital music distribution market. More and more new videos from providers or even individuals are getting on iTunes as well. Podcasts of new books also seek out iTunes first. The ability to attract these varied forms of digital content ensures a rich assortment of content for iTunes to offer to its users.

The other side of the market, that of the customer, is also well established. Many music lovers and owners of Apple devices know to come to iTunes first for their digital music needs. This makes iTunes a one-stop shop for listeners. As they spend time on iTunes, they learn about the other kinds of content that are available through the service. iTunes is also skilled at suggesting new content to users, based on the purchase behavior of previous users. So Apple can cross-sell a new kind of content to its customers based on its knowledge of their previous behavior. This exemplifies the economies of scope discussed in Chapter Four. And the presence of so many users ensures that the cycle will recur again, as new content will seek to be distributed on iTunes first.

The presence of this wealth of additional complementary investments greatly boosts the value of the platform for Apple. Yet Apple does not pay anything to induce these investments. Rather, others are investing money that will help Apple make more money. Perhaps the clearest example of this is the iFund, a dedicated fund of investment capital (initially $100 million and recently expanded to $200 million) launched by the venture capital firm Kleiner Perkins. The fund is focused on investment opportunities in Apple's devices, applications, and services. When an outside professional investment firm judges it to be a good financial move to dedicate a fund to growing your business platform, you know you have created a great business model.

Opening Up to Build a Platform

In two-sided markets, companies usually subsidize one side of the market in order to increase the attraction of the offering to the other side of the market.[15] So users pay no fee to register on iTunes, while content owners pay a percentage of their revenues to Apple in return for being distributed on iTunes (or the Apps store).

But this is not enough to establish the platform. The platform developer will need to broaden its business model planning beyond its own borders. In a platform business model, key suppliers and customers become business partners, entering into relationships in which both technical and business risk are shared. The business models of suppliers are now integrated into the planning processes of the company. The company in turn has integrated its business model into the business model of its key customers. And these customers share their future plans with the company, a critical part of their own business model. This allows the company to create its business model as a platform to lead its industry, including suppliers and customers.

This broadening of the business model must go still further. In addition to key suppliers and customers, many third parties that offer complementary products and services need to be encouraged to partic-ipate in the company's future business plans. These third parties could be current customers who share feedback with one another on their experiences, as well as recommendations for desired new services. They could be independent evaluators who are rating and reviewing services within the platform. They could be start-ups that are seeking to offer new possibilities to current customers. They could be individuals who have an inspiration for a new offering and want someone to try it and report back.

These outsiders need to be included in future planning. Companies need to reach out to them, work with them, and dedicate internal executives to providing the proper care and attention they need. Companies like the German software firm SAP, for instance, have senior managers with titles like vice president of ecosystems. These executives track the top contributors to the community around SAP's software. They provide kits and training to help customers and developers build additional offerings for the community and share information with outside researchers to help them understand trends within the community. SAP has even created a fund to invest in start-ups that are building software for the community. All of these are ways that a company can nurture the development and growth of its ecosystem.

One important device that enables this integration of business models throughout an ecosystem of suppliers, customers, partners, and collaborators is the ability of the company to establish its technologies as the basis for a platform of innovation for that ecosystem. In this way, the company can attract other companies into its business by sharing the tools, standards, intellectual property, and know-how needed for these supporting players to implement the platform successfully. This platform not only coordinates internal R&D with external R&D toward desired business objectives; it now shapes the future direction of that coordination.[16]

We have already seen this with TSMC's Open Innovation Platform from the previous chapter. Because TSMC has been a pioneer in the foundry business and still maintains the largest share of the foundry market, it is the firm best placed to coordinate the myriad technical activities in designing and manufacturing a variety of semiconductor chips. Not only can it develop its own tools and processes for others to use. It also attracts the tools, processes, and intellectual property of other companies. The investments of these other companies greatly increase the value of TSMC's processes to its customers. When customers are looking for the latest technologies for building new chips, they know that TSMC is likely to have them first, before the other foundries get them. They also know that the other foundries will have to copy TSMC's processes in order to remain competitive in the market so that the customers can start with TSMC now rather than wait until later for the other foundries. When the next generation of semiconductor manufacturing is being developed, TSMC is in a natural position to create the new generation architecture for how the chips will be manufactured.

Assembling the Open Services Innovation Concept Map

The way that the business model changes in services businesses completes the development of the concept map of this book that was introduced in Chapter One. Figure 5.3 shows the complete map again here for ease of reference.

Thinking of business as a service was discussed in Chapter Two, which featured the concepts of the services value chain, the utilization differential, and the importance of building a platform. The role of customers in co-creation was the focus of Chapter Three, where the concepts of tacit knowledge, experience points, and co-creation were examined. In Chapter Four, the economic forces underlying open innovation in services were presented. These concepts included the role of specialization, economies of scale and scope, and the integration of internal and external ideas and technologies through open innovation. This chapter has depicted the concepts of the business model, inertia in the business model, coherence among elements of the business model, and the importance of a platform business model.

FIGURE 5.3   Open Services Innovation Concept Map

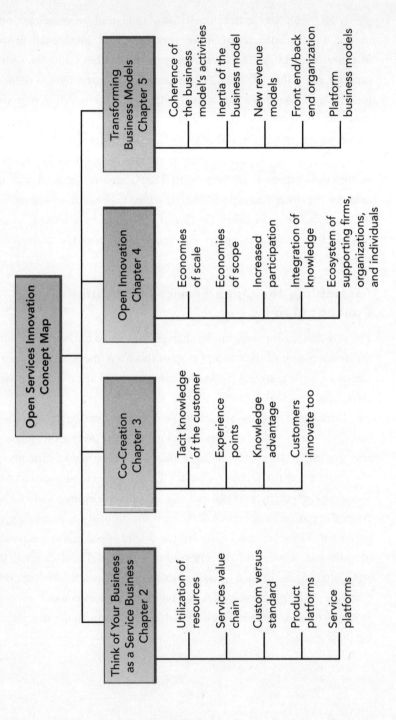

These concepts together provide the path away from the commodity trap. They point the way to how companies can prosper in a services-dominated economy, unlocking new sources of value for their customers and growth and profitability for themselves.

o o o

Now that we have examined all of the concepts of Open Services Innovation, it is time to see how they work in practice. The chapters in Part Two look at Open Services Innovation in a variety of different contexts, using the concept map in Figure 5.3 as a guide.

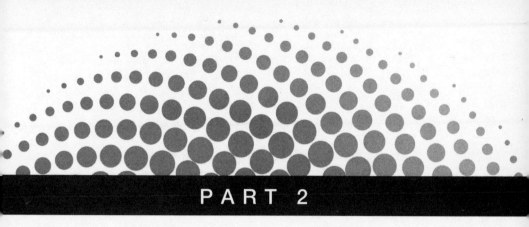

PART 2

OPEN SERVICES INNOVATION IN PRACTICE

This part starts with an examination of large organizations (Chapter Six) and then services innovation in smaller organizations (Chapter Seven). Innovation in services-based businesses is explored in more depth in Chapter Eight. I next move outside the United States and look at services innovation in developing economies (Chapter Nine). I conclude with some thoughts on the future direction of services innovation and what it means for policymakers and economic growth in society (Chapter Ten).

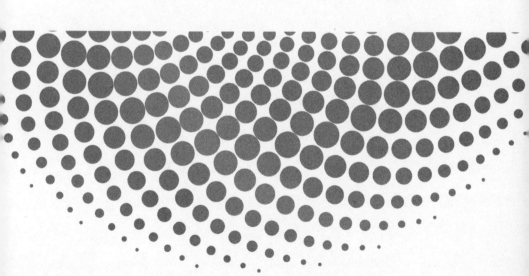

CHAPTER 6

OPEN SERVICES INNOVATION IN LARGER COMPANIES

This chapter looks at how services innovation is done by some organizations that have had real successes. In virtually every case, this success was born out of a series of challenges, failures, and experiments, for there is no easy way to innovate in services. It is hard work that brings with it risk, investment, and sometimes a little luck. Nevertheless, important lessons can be learned from companies that have been through this process and achieved success.

The organizations featured in this chapter come from a range of industries: copiers, airlines, industrial products, and financial services. I made these choices because the key learnings in services innovation are not, in my experience, related primarily to a particular industry but rather to the business model, the conception of the business, and the dominant logic used to make sense of the myriad inputs that every business must wrestle with.

XEROX

The first example of services innovation comes from an industrial powerhouse of the twentieth century, Xerox, that is now in the middle of a vital transition to a more services-oriented business.

Xerox has a proud tradition as the inventor of the xerographic process of copying images onto paper. It parlayed this invention into a multibillion-dollar business in the 1970s and remains a world leader in copiers and printers to this day. This endurance is all the more impressive for having to cope with a settlement decree with the Federal Trade Commission (FTC) in 1975 that required Xerox to license its core patents. The company encountered an enormous increase in competition (as intended by the FTC settlement), most of it from companies based in Japan (perhaps not intended by the FTC). Xerox's revenue share of the copier market fell from 80 percent in 1976 to 18 percent in 1982, which nearly sank the company. But Xerox fought back by making tremendous advances in the quality of its products and the technology used in them.

For the first forty years of its life, Xerox sold its copiers and printers as products. It charged for toner, paper, service, and often for financing the purchase of copiers as well. But these additional items were secondary (except for the toner, a key source of profits for the company) to the company's business model.

Today Xerox has embarked on an innovation of a different sort: an innovation in its business model for its copiers and printers. As Xerox looks for new sources of growth, it has become a far more services-oriented company, with more than 20 percent of its revenues in 2008 coming from services.[1] In particular, Xerox now offers a very different way for its customers to obtain copies: it owns and operates the copying and printing devices itself and charges customers only for their use. It calls this its "managed print services."

The managed print services offering is deceptively simple to offer but devilishly difficult to execute. The idea is that a company can sign a contract to have Xerox provide all of the copying services it needs. Xerox then takes responsibility for managing all of the copiers and printers in the company, keeping them up and running and properly maintained, replacing toner cartridges as required, and charging the company for the copies provided when they are provided. This is not an offer just for Xerox's own equipment; rather, the offer is for Xerox to manage all copiers and printers in the company, no matter their manufacturer, and wherever they are located.

From the customer's point of view, this is a beneficial arrangement. Managed print services convert what was a fixed cost into a variable cost for the customer, based on copy use. Customers therefore do not need to retain staff specialized in copying and printing functionality (as you might expect, there isn't much of a career path for such people in an organization, even though the specialized skills are definitely needed). So the customer can streamline its staffing and reduce its overheads associated with evaluating, selecting, procuring, installing, servicing, and financing its fleet of copiers. Procter & Gamble estimates that turning its fleet of copiers and printers over to Xerox will reduce its use of paper by 40 percent and cut its costs by 20 to 25 percent.[2]

This good deal for its customers is also beneficial for Xerox. The reasons involve many aspects of the ideas in this book. First, Xerox knows more about copiers and printers than even the most sophisticated of its customers, so its specialized knowledge allows it to manage resources more efficiently. Effective practices that Xerox observes in one managed service customer can readily be brought to bear at a second customer. Second, Xerox can develop, install, and operate the most efficient equipment over the life cycle of print services. For example, it often uses so-called multifunction devices that copy, print, fax, and scan. These are more expensive initially but last longer, use cheaper supplies, and perform more functions, so that more users can be serviced with fewer machines. This boosts the use of the equipment. Third, Xerox manages all of the print devices under these agreements, not just those of its own manufacture (openness again). Xerox therefore sees the entire organization's printing and copying needs.

Traditionally copiers and printers were purchased by a variety of functions within a company—information technology facilities, human resources, purchasing, and even individual employees—which resulted in a cacophony of devices around the organization. This dispersed equipment defeated the ability of any single equipment supplier to understand the needs of the overall organization. The managed print services model, by contrast, provides a unified view of all of the company's needs. It also provides deep knowledge of competitor product capabilities by supporting and servicing them daily. And it lets Xerox decide when to substitute its own devices for those of its competitors.

Finally, armed with this in-depth knowledge of its customers' print needs and experiences and competitor product capabilities and limitations, Xerox can create new generation systems. That will give it a learning advantage over its competitors that approach the business with more traditional market research techniques and have only a partial view of the organizations in which their machines are placed. Finally, the career path for people with deep knowledge of printers and their use is quite promising within Xerox, especially when compared to the career path of such a person inside one of its client organizations.

GE AVIATION

Services can also matter in traditional heavy industries. GE is a world leader in manufacturing aircraft engines. Such engines are not cheap: each costs $20 or 30 million or more. However, the market for new engines is competitive (Rolls Royce and Pratt and Whitney are strong competitors), and aircraft manufacturers are highly concentrated (Boeing and Airbus are the dominant customers). So it is hard for GE to make much money selling its engines. Instead, it looks to maintenance, spare parts, and financing as ways to make money from its engines once they are sold. This heavy industry manufacturer therefore makes most of its money from services, not the product. The product increasingly is just its way of acquiring customers to receive these services. As aircraft engine sales have leveled or fallen off, services have become an increasingly important part of GE Aviation's 2008 sales (25 percent of revenues) and profits (50 percent of profits).[3]

Like Xerox, GE has transformed its business model for its aircraft engines. In the past, each engine sale involved tens of millions of dollars, with a long sales cycle, lots of negotiations, and high-stakes bargaining. Yet most of the profit for GE from the engine comes not from its initial purchase, but rather from the services provided over the estimated thirty-year useful life of the engine.

This insight about the long tail of after-sale use prompted a shift in GE's business model for its engines.[4] GE's new model is "Power by the Hour," selling its engines much as a utility company might sell power to a residence or commercial enterprise.[5] GE will sell its engines for some thousands of dollars per operating hour, and the customer pays only when the plane is flying. Again, a large fixed cost for the customer is transformed into a variable cost instead.

This new model has an important second effect: better-aligned incentives. Both GE and its customers want to minimize the amount of downtime for unscheduled maintenance. Customers make no money from planes that are grounded for repairs, and under this new business model, GE doesn't make any money either. In fact, GE maintains a group of specialists who will fly anywhere in the world within twenty-four hours to repair a GE engine while it is still mounted on the wing of the plane (versus taking the engine off for repairs, which requires a tricky and time-consuming reinstallation process). They want to get that plane back in the air as quickly as possible, the same goal that GE's customers have.

These aligned incentives also stimulate GE to learn more about how to reduce unscheduled maintenance of its engines. Lessons that GE learns from servicing one engine are quickly shared with other GE technicians and engineers in order to prevent grounding another aircraft with that same engine for unscheduled maintenance, or to reduce the time needed for such maintenance to a minimum if the issue cannot wait until the next scheduled engine servicing. Across its fleet of engines, GE can develop sophisticated algorithms for predicting likely sources of future engine failure and the optimal time to service the engine to prevent such failures. The more data and experience GE accumulates, the better these algorithms become, and the more effective GE will become in delivering these services. Only a company with lots of data to work with can hope to do this well. This is a less appreciated knowledge-based economy of scale for GE.

GE also benefits from a third effect, one that reduces competition in the aftermarket for its spare parts and repair services. Most of the profit in an aircraft engine is derived from its thirty-year service life, but GE does not have this market to itself. A cottage industry of other companies that remanufacture GE parts and provide repair services has arisen around GE's engines. Many of the people who provide these services used to work as service technicians for GE, so they have been expertly trained on GE's engines.

The Power by the Hour business model is an important answer to this challenge. Third-party service companies cannot take on the responsibility to keep the planes flying the way GE can. Changing the pricing model for GE engines to this utility business model drives the repair business for GE's engines right back to GE itself. Of course, the customer could instead choose to buy the engine upfront for tens of millions of dollars and then find a third-party service organization that can maintain and repair the engine for less than GE would charge, but such an investment would pay back only in the very long term. And GE's fleet of technicians available around the clock on demand, along with the rapid knowledge transfer that arises from servicing the fleet of GE engines in service around the world, provides important knowledge advantages that third parties cannot obtain. In the long run, GE is likely to be able to reduce unscheduled maintenance of its engines to levels far below what third-party servicers could provide. Many GE customers therefore have opted for the variable-cost option of Power by the Hour instead.

As services have grown in importance to its business, GE has become more focused on organizing to exploit them. In 2005, GE created its OnPoint brand for all of its aviation services offerings. This allows the company to work with its customers across the range of services available and provide that one-stop shopping that we also saw with Xerox. GE thus realizes economies of scope through this process.

KLM ROYAL DUTCH AIRLINES

Most readers of this book are well acquainted with airports and probably feel that they spend too much time in them. Those who are old enough will have some mental comparison to an earlier time, where airplane travel was different (and thanks perhaps to nostalgia, regarded as somehow better). Few of us, though, have given much thought to how airplane travel changes over time. And on a cost basis per passenger mile at least, air travel is far better now than in earlier times.

KLM, the national carrier of the Netherlands, actually has three inter-related businesses. First, it is a worldwide airline, providing commercial passenger service to more than 250 destinations around the world. In 2004, it entered into a merger with Air France (and later with Air France in a transatlantic joint venture with Delta Airlines) but continues to operate under its own name. Second, it provides engineering and maintenance services for both its own aircraft and others (openness again). And finally, it provides cargo services to ship items along with passengers, or by full cargo planes, on its various routes (this last business does involve some inventory, namely the cargo in transit). But I focus here on its passenger airline business.

Innovation in an airline is a complex matter involving many different parties. At its root, however, are many of the considerations featured in this book. Airline services are consumed at the time that they are delivered; there is no inventory. This means that there is an immediacy that must be managed in making changes to the customer experience. And the customer's own choices (class of service; aisle, middle, or window seat; whether to check baggage; what meal; what beverage; what entertainment, whether to tilt back the seat; whether to use the tray table; and many others) influence the experience that the customer receives, so there is an element of co-creation involved as well.

This is where services innovation begins at KLM, with a new and distinctive view of the customer. As Ignaas Caryn, director of innovation and venturing at KLM, explains,

> If you look at KLM, let's say three or four years ago, we had defined our circle of contact with the customer, and that was really from the moment you came on the airport until you are at your destination, you have landed, and you left the airport and then you left KLM. Now we say well, there is still plenty of opportunity before that and after that—where we can offer value-added services to our customers, so we can extend our customer circle of contact. This is even more the case with new offerings we have developed concerning ancillary services such as hotel bookings, ground transportation services, online business communities, and so on, because they are really offering the whole package from door to door, minimizing the hassle for the customer. It can therefore be no

surprise that "customer experience" and "mobility and connectivity" are major innovation themes within KLM (a third one being "sustainable aviation").[6]

Another aspect of innovation for KLM is the extended service supply chain that the airline uses in providing its services. Of course, there are the airplane, the engines, and the airport. But a host of other providers are involved as well, particularly in areas that touch the customer: the catering of the food and drink, the cleaning service, the duty-free merchandise sold on the plane, and the entertainment electronics provided to the passengers, along with the content available for viewing using those electronics. Even the seats of the KLM plane are provided by external parties. So managing innovation at KLM involves both co-creation with customers and close cooperation with an extended chain of suppliers. Managing supply chains in a world of co-creation requires different processes for procuring suppliers' services. Caryn explains:

> If you look also at KLM, let's say ten years ago, we had this traditional procurement process where we wanted to have a supplier for the lowest price. What we would do is negotiate everything to get to the lowest price. That was the kind of relationship we had. If you really think that you need to work together to be innovative and you need these companies in your innovation process, then you also have to alter your procurement process.... It has to be altered from a purely cost-based discussion to a partnership discussion.... The mental attitude about procurement has to change, which does not happen overnight, but at least within KLM, we see very positive changes in the past few years....
>
> An example is the development of lightweight equipment such as baggage containers, in-flight trolleys, and cargo pallets. Lightweight equipment (produced from composites instead of aluminum) has many advantages: lower weight, of course (thus, less fuel consumption and carbon dioxide emission), facilitating the use of RFID [radiofrequency identification], process automation for baggage and cargo handling, better labor conditions, and so on. However, it took a long time before these developments got focus because in a traditional setting, a supplier having invested in aluminum production lines is not keen to invest in costly R&D and new production lines if not knowing that at least one customer will buy its new stuff; sales might prove difficult due to the

initially higher sales price, although a positive impact on the TCO [total cost of ownership] can be projected.

On the other side, an airline will not accept new equipment if this has not been severely tested, certified, complies with required specifications, and so on. To solve this dilemma, KLM, a concept engineering start-up, and an airline equipment supplier engaged in a co-creation mode to co-create composite equipment, with KLM as launching customer. [As in the Xerox and GE examples, a shift from a fixed to a variable cost is taking place, leading to a better alignment of incentives between KLM and its supplier.]

KLM now also wants to transfer this partnership experience to its marketing environment for the further development of its online business communities (such as Club China, Club Africa, and Golf Club). These communities offer customers valuable location-based information, local services, interesting discounts (for example, on golf courses), access to a network of other businesspeople, and so on. Although its customers value these kind of extra services very much, KLM is not an expert in building and growing successful online communities. The solution was to team up with a young, innovative marketing company.

Again, this company benefits from KLM as launching customer, and KLM will benefit not only from the expertise of its supplier and increased added value of its communities to its customers, but also from the future potential value increase of this company as it intends to sign an option deal with this company. This means both companies envisage cooperating for a longer period and understand the value of such longer-term cooperation (or co-creation).

So costs remain critically important, but pursuing innovation in services requires treating suppliers in a different way. Taking a partnership approach shifts the focus away from pushing down prices to identifying solutions that either reduce costs in the system (while maintaining margins) or deliver an enhanced experience to the final customer. Often the partner will have detailed, valuable knowledge to contribute. But if the airline is going to extract all of the profit for itself, the supplier has no incentive to share its valuable knowledge with the airline customer. This kills innovation from the supply chain.

One of the major players in KLM's service delivery is its home base, Schiphol, Amsterdam's airport. The accessibility of the airport, car parking, check-in (although this one is increasingly done by mobile phone), baggage drop-off, security control, communication and services at the airport, congestion of air traffic, and so on: all of these influence the customer experience. Therefore, many innovations need to be developed in close cooperation with the airport. This was one of the reasons that KLM and Schiphol engaged in the Mainport Innovation Fund (other partners are the Delft University of Technology, with its renowned aerospace faculty, and Rabobank). Caryn says:

> This seed capital fund invests in innovative start-ups developing technology and/or services related to aviation, airlines, and/or airports. The setting of the fund partners is not randomly chosen, as each of the partners brings a specific competency: launching customer and offering business knowledge (KLM and Schiphol), a window on technology and experience with start-ups (TU Delft and its incubator Yes!Delft), and financial/investment expertise (Rabobank).
>
> The start-up benefits from the fund investment and launching customer potential, and KLM benefits (directly) from accelerated innovation and (indirectly by the fund) from the value increase of the start-up.

This is where service innovations are born: through a deep understanding of the customer and of customer needs that are currently unmet, on the one hand, and from intensive cooperation with suppliers, on the other hand. Notice that Caryn is not imposing the utilization of KLM's fleet of aircraft and major airports and route structures on the situation. He is starting from his understanding of the business traveler's need for a hassle-free, seamless travel experience and, with the relevant suppliers, formulating his business around that insight.

The service thinking does not stop there. Once the executive has disembarked from the plane at the airport, how does he get to the meeting? Caryn notes:

> A service that very nicely connects to our business travelers is a global car service, a car with driver. A service that you can book and pay in advance in combination with your KLM ticket. This saves the traveler the hassle of long waiting lines, the need for foreign currency, dealing with dubious

taxi drivers, and expenses reporting once back home. For corporate travel managers, it offers more transparency in travel costs.

To set up this service, we engaged with a start-up company, both commercially as well as through an option deal. This company has contracted in the most important cities in the United States, Europe, and Asia with high-quality local car service providers. So they look at different suppliers and choose one per city. They then combine the KLM distribution channels with their service provider network. For KLM to build up this service itself would be a real challenge, as it requires different competencies and focus in the concept development and day-to-day execution. These are better covered with the a different company. However, KLM acting as a launching customer brings tremendous value to this company, not only by opening up its own distribution network but also by introducing this company to other airlines within the SkyTeam alliance [SkyTeam is the broader airline alliance to which KLM belongs].

KLM seeks to provide an entire travel experience to its business clients, from the time they book their services, prepare their journey, and leave their house, to their arrival at their business destination, and back. KLM does not expect to provide all of the service itself; rather it will orchestrate a suite of service experiences for clients using a network of service suppliers and partners, as described above with the taxi services.

The answer to the question of whether this provides a competitive advantage to KLM is yes and no. Yes, these initiatives differentiate KLM for a period of time, until others copy or imitate what it is doing. After that, no, they do not. But if KLM can develop additional innovations and deploy those ahead of its competitors, then its customers will enjoy services that they cannot yet find on competing airlines. A succession of temporary advantages for KLM can differentiate the company against its competition. I'll give Caryn the last word on this: "No competitive advantage in this environment is long term, but as long as we can provide continuous innovation, we can win."

MERRILL LYNCH

At this writing, the financial services industry has been devastated by the implosion of the mortgage-backed securities market, followed by the even more devastating collateralized debt swap fiasco. Bank capital has been severely depleted, and banks lack functioning markets to price realistically the assets that they hold. This situation makes it challenging to talk about innovation in the financial sector since the current disaster can be viewed as innovation run amok. However, after the mess is finally cleaned up, the financial sector will remain an important sector. In addition, it has seen many helpful service innovations in the past two decades that are worth understanding and will undoubtedly survive the current crisis.

Daniel Fasnacht, in his book *Open Innovation in the Financial Services Industry*, details a variety of helpful innovations that have arisen in this important part of the services sector.[7] One innovation I discuss relates to Merrill Lynch and its business model innovation for managing its clients' assets and portfolios.[8]

Back more than twenty years ago, a schism erupted in the stock brokerage industry. Upstarts like Charles Schwab began to offer discount trading services, allowing customers to trade stocks with a much smaller commission being paid to the stockbroker. As stock market information became more widely disseminated, brokers no longer needed a seat on the exchange to execute the trade, and so consumers were now able to trade stocks much more affordably. This coincided with a rapid increase in trading activity by individual investors versus the more traditional trading activity of institutional investors.

This more affordable way to trade stocks, however, created some big headaches for the traditional full-service brokerage firms like Merrill Lynch.[9] These firms maintained extensive networks of stockbrokers who served customers with personal attention, providing stock trading tips to customers, and relaying trading orders back to headquarters for execution of the trades. They made their money by charging a commission on each stock trade. This high-service model was now directly threatened by the rise of the discount brokers, who charged much less to make trades.

To make matters worse, another innovation came into the broad financial market: the rise of mutual funds and index funds. Instead of trading individual stocks, increasingly trading volumes were shifting to these funds, which were baskets of stocks. Funds that performed unusually well, such as Peter Lynch's Magellan Fund at Fidelity, attracted hundreds of thousands of investors and billions of dollars of capital. And John Bogle of Vanguard was convincing many investors to invest in mutual index funds that tracked the performance of certain types of assets, such as the S&P 500 or the Russell 2000.

As such mutual funds and index funds became more widely known and accepted, the prospects for hot stock tips from one's local broker became less compelling. This, combined with the concomitant rise of discount brokers, triggered a crisis for full-service brokers like Merrill Lynch. With the overheads associated with a large network of brokers providing personalized service to their clients in a world of falling commissions—and rising mutual fund purchases—how Merrill Lynch could remain a value-added financial partner for its clients was a real dilemma.

To make matters worse for Merrill Lynch, innovation in financial services is problematic because of the weak intellectual property protection for innovations in the industry. Successful initiatives are quickly copied, with the pioneer unable to appropriate much, if any, advantage for taking the risks to develop it first.[10]

Notwithstanding these considerable problems, Merrill Lynch's answer to its dilemma stemmed directly from innovation in the financial services sector. This innovation did not happen all at once, and not all of its initiatives succeeded. And like KLM, Merrill's successful innovations provided only a temporary advantage. Nevertheless, a series of advantages can provide a significant leg up over a considerable period of time.

One important innovation in the 1980s that helped Merrill substantially in its increasingly difficult environment was the innovation of its cash management account, an account that swept all available cash in a client's account every day and invested it in short-term money market funds on behalf of the client. In this way, Merrill assured its customers that their money was always working for them. And the sweeping of each account spared customers the headache of having to track residual amounts of money left over in each account after trades were made to be sure that they were being invested in income-generating assets.

This innovation was highly popular and therefore widely imitated. But Merrill got there first and had it to itself for a short period of time. Other innovations that Merrill initiated were copied from others. It launched its own mutual funds and recruited money managers with good reputations to manage these funds. Then it actively marketed these funds as part of its clients' portfolios.

These innovations created a situation in which Merrill was potentially conflicted in terms of its work with its clients. On the one hand, the Merrill broker was a trusted broker for his or her client and charged with providing the best, most objective investment advice possible. On the other hand, the Merrill broker was a distribution channel for Merrill's own mutual funds. The more money that was invested with these funds, the more profitable they would be for Merrill. Clients therefore could not always be sure that the Merrill broker had their interests foremost in mind.[11] Merrill often restricted access to its funds to its own clients, though it later opened up its funds for sale to others as well.

Because of these concerns, and because it was costly to initiate new mutual funds (the demand for such funds was uncertain and might therefore take a long time before attracting enough investors to make money), Merrill also began offering third-party mutual funds in another example of a broader economy of scope in services intended to facilitate one-stop shopping for Merrill's clients. This allowed Merrill to provide a full selection of mutual funds (even index funds) to its clients, whether they were managed by Merrill or a third party. These efforts, however, were barely keeping Merrill ahead of the discount brokers. Many mutual funds were happy to sell through Schwab, and later even more bare-bones brokers, like E-Trade and TD Waterhouse, emerged.

In the 1990s, Merrill hit on a new business model to differentiate itself more fully from the discount brokers and stay ahead of them: the asset management business model. This model differed fundamentally from the brokerage model in how money was earned. Broker models charged commissions per trade in order to make money, so more trading activity led to more profit for the broker. More than a few clients felt that their Merrill brokers were trying to get them to trade more often in order to keep the commissions flowing. Asset management altered the revenue model: managers receive a percentage of assets in the account under management as a fee regardless of the volume of trading in that account.

This model had been in existence in private banking for a long time, but Merrill was the first national broker to bring it to the large customer base that it had established. Charging a fee of 1 percent of assets under management, Merrill did away with brokerage commissions on stock trades for its clients who signed up. The Merrill brokers changed their title, and indeed their function: they were now called Merrill financial advisors.

Notice the impact this had on the earlier potential for conflicts of interest. Previously clients needed to be concerned that they were being steered into specific funds that Merrill owned or steered into more frequent trades than they wished to make in order to generate revenue for the broker. With the asset management model, Merrill financial advisors made money on the amount of money under management in the account.[12] If the account grew in value, the financial advisor received more money. Now the incentives of the Merrill advisor were better aligned with those of its clients.

This innovation has provided a more enduring advantage for Merrill. It created a meaningful differentiation from the discount brokers (who did not, and could not, provide financial advice to their clients) and insulated Merrill from the commission wars where some brokers were offering trades for under ten dollars. Until its merger with Bank of America on January 1, 2009 (as a result of the financial implosion in collateralized debt obligations that were one of the "innovations" noted at the beginning of this chapter), Merrill enjoyed a prolonged period of high profitability as a result of its switch to the asset management business model.

LESSONS FROM SERVICES INNOVATION IN LARGE COMPANIES

If we step back from the individual companies, we can see some patterns that recur across a diverse group of companies and industries. These patterns reinforce the key themes in this book, so it is worth examining them again here to see where the themes apply in more detail.

One theme that emerges from these individual large organizations is the role of tacit information (derived from experience), which is quite important in services. This requires coordination between the supplier of the service and the customer to elicit this hard-to-articulate knowledge. In financial services, for example, the needs of the client for his or her portfolio play an important role in what investments make sense. And clients' needs, risk preferences, and need for cash vary over their lives as well. This is information that discount brokerages cannot access because of their very low-cost trading commission model. It is information that takes time, conversation, and the creation of a certain level of trust to elicit. Merrill's financial advisors are better positioned to access this kind of information and can offer a differentiated set of services to clients as a result.

In a different way, both GE and Xerox also have positioned themselves to access this more tacit form of knowledge. By taking responsibility for keeping the engine flying as much as possible, GE gains access to the entire maintenance history of the engine. It can even position sensors on the engines to log specific operating parameters and detect whenever key parameters (as temperature, thrust, fuel consumption, and so on) are out of their normal range. These exception indicators may signal the need for immediate servicing or in other cases may signal an additional repair to be undertaken at the next servicing. By taking over the entire fleet of copiers, including those of its competitors, Xerox's managed print services let it observe the use of a variety of copiers throughout the many different parts of its customers' operations. Xerox can also develop measures for predictive maintenance and preventive maintenance. It can gain further insight into the actual use of copiers and printers in different areas and develop new products with these insights in mind, among them features that reduce lifetime installation, operation, and service costs, which make the managed print services offerings more profitable for Xerox.

A second important theme is co-creation. KLM is working hard to enable its customers to co-create their flying experience with KLM. Customers now have an array of choices available to them in booking the flight and in what activities and services they consume during that flight. KLM also must co-create with its extensive supply chain in order to provide this widening array of choices to its customers. Moreover, the airline is taking a customer-centric view of its services, so that it can identify unmet needs among certain segments of its market. This broader view of customers' travel needs, from the moment they begin planning the trip to the moment they leave for the airport, through to the time they arrive at their final destination, enables possible new services to be envisioned.

Merrill's financial advisors necessarily must co-create with their clients. Clients must sign off on recommendation investments, and they must advise Merrill on key life events that might trigger a shift in the investment portfolio. Clients talk to friends and coworkers and read the financial press, and they often have ideas of their own for possible investments. Competing financial services providers also can try to lure some portion of a client's investment activity to them instead of Merrill. Merrill advisors, in turn, are exposed to a wealth of information that is not apparent to most clients. This information is a key source of expertise that they provide to clients. So both advisor and client co-create the investment strategy and manage the resulting portfolio.

A third theme, which GE and Xerox exemplify directly, is the role of business models in services innovation. Both have transformed their business models in ways that convert their business from one that makes products to one that delivers services (services that, to be sure, are anchored by products and technologies). And their service-oriented business model broadens the scope of activities that each undertakes on behalf of clients. This is also true of Merrill Lynch's switch from a brokerage model to an asset management model. Managing a client's portfolio requires much greater knowledge of key life events in a client's life: marriage, divorce, college education, estate planning, and so on.

A final theme is the role of openness in services innovation. Openness enables service innovators to achieve economies of both scale and scope. Merrill Lynch offered third-party mutual funds, broadening the number of fund choices available to its clients. KLM offers third-party arrangements for ground transportation and cooperates intensively with the airport to improve the customer experience. Xerox manages all copiers and printers at its customers' locations, regardless of manufacturer. These are all examples of economies of scope that derive from a willingness to include third parties in the service offering.

By offering managed print services to its customers, Xerox sees more machines (from a variety of manufacturers) over more time than others who simply maintain their own machines. GE knows more about its engines throughout their useful lives through its Power by the Hour business model. Merrill Lynch's financial advisors now watch their clients' entire portfolios rather than individual stocks. These economies of scale confer meaningful knowledge advantages, in addition to simply spreading fixed costs more widely. So leaders like Xerox, GE, and Merrill Lynch are likely to develop even better solutions for their customers in the future.

o   o   o

The examples in this chapter are all from rather large organizations. How service innovation, and the themes in this book, apply to smaller organizations is the focus of the next chapter.

CHAPTER 7

OPEN SERVICES INNOVATION IN SMALLER COMPANIES

This chapter considers how services innovation operates in smaller firms. Both the economies of scale and scope from services innovation are presumably more difficult to achieve for smaller organizations. Moreover, smaller firms lack the resources and often lack strong protection of their intellectual property that large firms typically enjoy.

The issue here is how small and medium-sized firms (SMEs) can manage these constraints in services innovation. This is not just an important theoretical question. Notwithstanding the power of many large firms, SMEs are of growing importance for an economy's innovative capacity. They have increased their R&D budget faster than the largest firms and now play an increasingly important role in national innovation systems.[1] Whether the consideration is jobs, patents, or R&D spending, SMEs as a group are winning against large firms.

Figure 7.1 shows the growing importance of small firms in industrial R&D spending during the past twenty-six years in the United States. Large firms with more than twenty-five thousand employees were responsible for 70 percent of the industrial R&D spending in 1981. Their share fell by half, to 35 percent, in 2007. In contrast, small firms with fewer than one thousand employees increased their share from 4 percent to 24 percent

---

This chapter is based in part on an unpublished paper with two of my academic colleagues, Oliver Gassmann and Wim Vanhaverbeke: "How Smaller Companies Can Benefit from Open Innovation" (January 2009).

133

FIGURE 7.1   U.S. Industrial R&D by Firm Size

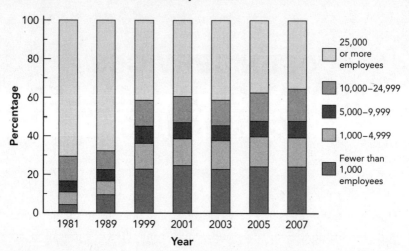

Source: National Science Foundation, Science Resource Studies, *Survey of Industrial Research Development* (1999, 2001, 2003, 2006, 2008).

during that period. Large firms are still very important in industrial R&D because their share is still big (35 percent) and their amount of R&D spending increased from $21.2 billion in 1981 to $94.8 billion in 2007, a factor of four. The increase in R&D expenditures by small firms was even more impressive: those with fewer than one thousand employees spent $64.7 billion in 2007 compared to $1.3 billion in 1981, a factor of fifty. In other words, smaller firm R&D spending overall has grown ten times as fast as that of large company spending over these twenty-six years.

FIGURING OUT WHERE YOUR BUSINESS FITS

A small business cannot be all things to all people, so its leaders must know where to compete and how to compete. Two dimensions help characterize the opportunities available in an industry for a small business. One important dimension is the scale of R&D required to develop technologies in an industry. Some industries feature substantial economies of scale, among them petrochemical refining, semiconductor manufacturing, pharmaceutical development, and mass market retailing. Other

FIGURE 7.2   Types of SMEs (Small and Medium-Sized Firms)

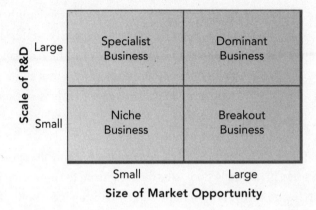

Size of Market Opportunity

industries do not exhibit these economic requirements, such as the toy industry, the medical device industry, and the fashion industry.

The second dimension to consider is the size of the market opportunity. Technology markets typically evolve through a life cycle, starting small, progressing rapidly in a growth phase, plateauing in a mature phase, and then declining at the end-of-life phase. So at the beginning and end of the cycle, markets are relatively small in size. Conversely, in the middle phases, market size has become quite large.

Combining these two dimensions yields the two-by-two matrix shown in Figure 7.2. The innovation opportunities available to SMEs are determined by the position of the firm in this matrix.

NICHE BUSINESSES

In the niche business quadrant, the economies of scale in R&D are small, and market size is also small. Many, perhaps most, SMEs are found in this quadrant. Typically they have started with a limited budget in a small niche market. As long as they stay focused on a niche market, they stay small and, if they are sufficiently skilled, relatively comfortable. Here the scale of R&D investment is small, while the market opportunity is likewise going to be small. But service firms in these niches can still improve their businesses through services innovation. A sailing club in Berkeley, California, illustrates this point well.

The Olympic Circle Sailing Club

Anthony Sandberg loves to sail.[2] After a number of years in other kinds of business, he realized that his life would be more satisfying if he learned how to turn his avocation into his livelihood. Since he had sailed in a number of places in a variety of boats, he knew a great deal about how to sail. His many sailing excursions had also given him extensive experience with marinas, sailing organizations, teaching schools, and other sailors.

Sandberg wanted to have a good marina, a variety of boats for sailing, and some top-notch classes to teach people how to enjoy the sport safely. But he wanted his sailing school to be different from the others: he wanted his clients to find a sense of community and friendship in his sailing school.

After a couple of false starts, he found a wonderful location on the coast of the San Francisco Bay in Berkeley, California. The marina was located in a protected area of the bay, behind a large water break. It had views up and down the bay and looked out directly at the island of Alcatraz and the Golden Gate Bridge. The facilities, however, were decidedly in need of help. The buildings were decrepit, some of the boats were rotting in place, the facility had previously been a landfill, and the harbor needed to be dredged.

Sandberg founded the Olympic Circle Sailing Club in 1979, and his partner, Richard Jepson, joined him the next year. Initially the two founders led many of the classes themselves. With the passage of time and the helpful advice of a business partner, they learned that they could recruit excellent teachers who were every bit as qualified to instruct as they were. This freed up their time to work more on the business side of the sailing club, now called the OCSC.[3]

Sandberg wanted to share his love of sailing with others, so with his additional time, he began to seek newcomers to sailing to come to his club and learn how to sail. The sailing club became approved by the United States Sailing Association, so that clients who completed his courses would be certified to sail at other clubs that also belonged to the association. Sandberg was careful to offer the newcomers all of the basic gear for rental or for purchase, so they could have a one-stop experience in getting lessons on the boat. Once the customers had completed the appropriate classes, they could charter boats themselves.

The sailing was great, lots of people took classes, the facilities were gradually upgraded over time, the boats were replaced, the harbor was dredged, and the OCSC began to expand. But the business wasn't very profitable. In fact, if Sandberg paid himself appropriately for all the time he was working at the club, it would have been unprofitable. He began to seek outside advice to figure out what he should be doing.

With the help of some outside advisors (who did not charge him for their advice, but instead received complimentary boat rentals and trips), he learned what his various services were costing him and what gear customers were willing to pay for. As it happened, in his desire to supply everything clients would want for sailing, he had too much inventory that sold far too little (such as all kinds of foul weather gear and many kinds of maps) and not enough gear that customers always wanted but were out of stock (such as ear warmers, gloves, eyeglass holders, and sunscreen).

He also learned that many sailors drop out after taking classes and renting boats for a year or two, so he had to figure out how to sustain their interest for a longer period of time. The key, he realized, was to strengthen the sense of community within the OCSC in order to give clients a social connection to sailing. As an example, OCSC's boats start at twenty-four feet in length, and most boats of that size or longer have at least two people on board to operate, so sailing often requires getting at least two people together for the sail.

Armed with these insights, Sandberg transformed OCSC from a sailing school into a sailing club, though one that still offered classes. It charged membership fees, so that its revenues now came primarily from club members, not from classes (members received a discount on the classes, giving new sailors an incentive to join the club). The classes were now simply a means to expand the membership of the club and serve the members.

Then the challenge became how to extend the natural length of members' interests so that they remained engaged for a longer period of time. One choice was to offer free refresher courses to members every spring, so that they would feel confident and safe taking out boats as the rains stopped and the lovely spring weather began. Another choice was to put on regular events at the club for members to gather and socialize. One event might be for organizing a flotilla to the British Virgin Islands:

members would fly to the islands and charter a group of boats together. Another might be seeing pictures from a recent excursion to the Galápagos Islands as motivation for joining a future trip there. A favorite event was Wednesday night sails in summer, followed by a barbecue at the club.

A major innovation investment was to create an online system for members to identify themselves, their level of expertise, the kinds of sailing they like to do, and the dates on which they would be available to sail. Someone wanting to charter a boat, for example, could send out a request to the other members, filtering for these criteria. Those who met the criteria would receive an e-mail and have the opportunity to reply if they were interested and available. This system made it much easier for members to find each other, share the rental fees, and sail more often. It helped the business in two ways: it increased the number of boat rentals from members and gave members more reason to keep paying their monthly dues.

A further business insight was that OCSC did not have to own the boats to hire them out. Sailboats are a classic underused asset. In fact, an old aphorism widely shared within the sailing community is, "The two happiest days in a sailor's life are the day he buys his boat, and the day he sells it." Most sailors who own boats use them infrequently, with the cost of the boat, its slip, its maintenance, and upkeep constant drains on the sailor's finances (hence the "second happiest day" in the aphorism above). OCSC now acts as an agent for the boat owner, letting its members charter the boat while splitting the revenue from the rental with the owner. OCSC also keeps the boat maintained for the owner while in the slip, so that the boat remains in top operating condition for the owner and ready for a sail. This system dramatically reduces the fixed assets needed to operate the sailing club, since the cost of each boat starts at $25,000 for a twenty-four footer, going up to $300,000 or more for boats over forty feet. By acting as an agent, OCSC can offer members a choice of nearly fifty boats without burdening its balance sheet with the high fixed costs of acquiring those boats.

As a result of these innovations, OCSC has successfully righted itself and become a healthy business. Members get to know one another, many friendships form as a result of sailing together, and members stay in the club for a longer period of time than in the past. Having more members makes it feasible to rent more boats more often, and Sandberg now knows the kinds of gear that sailors will pay for to enjoy their trips. There are groups that congregate to sail together elsewhere: in Turkey, the British Virgin Islands, or the Galápagos. And through it all, Sandberg's love of sailing is undiminished: he now does what he loves for a much more profitable living.

Lessons for Services Firms in Niche Businesses

OCSC demonstrates some of the concepts already explored in this book. One idea is the one-stop shopping that the club provides for its sailing members. When a member wants to organize an outing, the club helps him or her find additional sailors and provides the gear, maps, and even amenities like sunscreen and lip balm, along with lessons in sailing. Another is the idea of leveraging the utilization advantage of aggregating members together on the one side and managing a fleet of owners' boats on the other side. A third is the use of events and online communities to get members together, so that the members co-create their membership experience, thereby extending their time as members in the club.

These kinds of opportunities for smaller firms in niche positions also bring risks to consider. One is the risk of obsolescence: a focused company in a niche risks being blindsided by unforeseen developments. Because OCSC was able to obtain its privileged position with only a modest amount of R&D investment, its competitors also typically can enter at low cost. In addition, niche businesses typically find that their customers have low switching costs to embrace alternative suppliers when a better technology comes along. Sandberg has some protection against this obsolescence due to the relatively few spots on the bay where sailing operations can be located. But if there were a sudden swing in popularity toward, say, windsurfing, that could damage his business.

Another risk is that of weak protection for an SME's intellectual property. A company may work closely with a customer only to find that the customer over time has either designed the offering out of the system or has developed a substitute offering internally or from a third party.

Because the niche firm is small by design, it lacks the resources to address this weakness effectively.

Happily OCSC is not a business that depends on exclusive intellectual property. It takes care to be certified by the U.S. Sailing Association, but its activities and practices do not revolve around intellectual property. And its unique location and Sandberg's obvious love of sailing are difficult resources for others to copy as well.

BREAKOUT BUSINESSES

Some service businesses start small and then catch fire as their market begins to grow much, much larger. Such businesses face a different set of innovation challenges from the niche businesses due to the rapid growth they encounter. These become breakout businesses (see Figure 7.2).

NetBase

Jonathan Spier and Michael Osofsky run NetBase, a company that finds itself squarely in the middle of a breakout business. They met as undergraduate students in computer science at the University of California, Berkeley. Each was interested in artificial intelligence (AI) and how computers could be used to uncover knowledge and meaning from various kinds of data. Spier decided to pursue a path in management by going to the Harvard Business School, while Osofsky, who has a passion for innovation, received an M.B.A. from MIT's Sloan School of Management.

Because of their friendship, mutual respect, and shared interests, they determined to start a business where they could work together. They knew it would be related to their shared background in AI, but they also knew that earlier-generation companies in AI had largely been unsuccessful. There had been too much hype, too little understanding of business problems, and an inability to match the promise of the technology to the reality of the marketplace. Spier and Osofsky therefore focused on starting a company with a business vision of helping to drive innovation based on understanding market needs and matching them to solutions.

They launched their business, initially called Accelovation, in 2004. As the name implied, they were going to use the power of computer technology to help companies accelerate innovation far more effectively. They thought that new product development could be an area where their technology could help, since companies had to process a great deal of information about market needs, product requirements, and gaps that were unfilled in the market in order to get new products out the door faster.

Their aim was also ambitious. They did not wish to solve the problems of a few customers as consultants. They were hoping to solve problems at enough companies that they could grow into a successful organization that one day might go public or otherwise create significant value for its investors. For this reason, they accepted outside financing from Thomvest and Altos Ventures, which were looking for the company to generate a handsome return on their investment.

As Spier and Osofsky began their work, they started looking for early customers who needed their technology and would provide some revenue and, more important, help them see how customers applied their technology actually inside organizations. They did the searches for early customers themselves because they believed it was important to understand the customer problem deeply before attempting to produce new, complex technology for mass use.

Over time Spier and Osofsky discovered an initial market opportunity for their technology: managing intellectual property (IP) in the science, technology, and medical publishing markets. Companies often own lots of patents, trademarks, and copyrights, but they typically lack much understanding of what the value these IP assets might be. A semantic search tool could help companies understand better their own IP and the IP of others, including competitors. Accelovation began to attend meetings of The Gathering, a group of managers interested in improving the way in which IP is organized.

Spier and Osofsky were successful in working with two of the top three largest science and technology publishers in the world, but the business (it changed its name to NetBase in 2008) did not grow as rapidly as they had expected. Nevertheless, the relationships that the company formed were helpful in getting some customer wins, and through those wins, Spier and Osofsky developed more relationships to learn how their semantic search technology was used inside companies. Consumer product companies like Procter & Gamble, for example, were using NetBase to research technology landscapes. NetBase was helping them eliminate unpromising products while identifying the most promising market opportunities for development and improving their overall research processes.

Then a new market application for the technology, netnography, or social media understanding, emerged at the request of one of NetBase's customers, who then helped recruit five of the top ten consumer product companies. Netnography is the use of semantic search (or linguistic understanding) on the Web to scour consumer blogs, Twitter and Facebook accounts, and all kinds of consumer-generated content for insights about consumers' likes and dislikes, emotions, and behaviors around brands. Instead of relying on traditional market research technologies to identify consumer needs and perceptions, netnography enables companies to see what consumers are saying themselves in their own words and their own chosen setting. It is much more authentic than traditional market research techniques like focus groups and surveys and much faster to probe.

Leveraging this netnography tool, called ConsumerBase, has allowed NetBase to focus its marketing activities far more precisely. Unlike the earlier companies in artificial intelligence, there is less hype, and the technology is now under the hood, not front and center, in sales pitches.

NetBase has a focused business now. It serves the market research and brand management function at the largest brands in the world. In addition, it is partnering with market research firms and advertising and digital agencies, as well as other technology companies. According to customers, NetBase is changing the way market research is done and doing it faster, cheaper, and in the most natural habitat for gaining authentic consumer insight.

The challenges here are that netnography's potential is too great to be served by one small but growing company. Other companies are now moving into the space, and competition is growing. NetBase is off to a strong start in this new market, with impressive success to date, but the company has a way to go before it delivers the payday that its founders and investors are hoping for.

Lessons for Services Firms in Breakout Businesses

The large market opportunity puts many SMEs at considerable risk when they want to seize large market opportunities. In most cases, enlarging the business requires a revision, and maybe more than one, of the business model. Of course, there is no guarantee that a business model innovation will succeed. NetBase's model has evolved at least a couple of times in its search for a large market. Access to investment capital to enable the company to finance its growth is also vital, since breakout businesses typically grow faster than their initial capital allows them to do (in contrast to niche businesses). NetBase has raised significant funds from professional investors on attractive terms so far. Nevertheless, such capital can be tough to come by for small businesses, especially in hard times.

Growing beyond a niche also requires a search for external partners in the value chain (or ecosystem) to break out from its niche market. Attracting external partners and managing them effectively is an important skill as well, something that OCSC has not had to worry about.

NetBase has had good success so far in its partnership with one of the world's leading publishing companies, Elsevier. But Elsevier, like every other partner, may choose to change its model down the road or switch to a different provider of semantic search technology, a risk that NetBase must manage.

Indeed, managing partners can be hazardous for breakout businesses. The RISC microprocessor architecture of MIPS Computer Systems is an example (though this is a product, not a service). In the 1990s, MIPS, a small start-up company, became a potential threat for Intel's microprocessors in the PC market. MIPS could become so powerful thanks to its large network of partners, including chip manufacturers, PC vendors, value-added resellers, and software companies. However, as the alliance network grew, it became so large that it was no longer manageable for the start-up. Conflicts of interest between partners weakened the network.

When two of the members, DEC and Compaq, announced that they were reducing support for their MIPS-based systems, that small announcement triggered a cascade that caused the other partners eventually to withdraw from the MIPS initiative. That sunk the company.[4]

A network of partners can allow small companies to become stronger competitors, but they require strong network management by the small firm. If the smaller firm does not know how to manage the network, its strength rapidly turns into a liability, which in most cases leads to bankruptcy or takeover by one of the alliance partners. One important lesson firms can draw from the MIPS example is that small networks are much easier to manage than large ones.[5]

Openness plays a decisive role in breakout businesses. It enables smaller firms to achieve leverage in the market by harnessing the efforts of many others not on its payroll in order to mobilize the resources needed to pursue the opportunity. In the Internet computer industry, several smaller services firms (Netflix, Facebook, MySpace, and Twitter, for example) became global players by getting into the breakout business with a new business model. Different strategies lead to a breakout business for SMEs, but all have in common that they leveraged their external resources extensively in innovations for their business model.

SPECIALIST SERVICE BUSINESSES

In some businesses with small market opportunities but large R&D requirements, specialist service firms have exciting opportunities. For example, engineering and scientific businesses that require technical services face large investments in R&D. In this situation, the market opportunity is small, so specialist firms can develop attractive businesses without fear of being overtaken by much larger firms. The smaller market opportunity protects them from as much competition as that faced by breakout service businesses.

Another example of specialist service firms comes in the area of innovation services. When large companies have to cut back internal R&D spending, they compensate in part by developing innovation services to spot, understand, and in-license promising external innovations quickly. In industries with few economies of scale in developing new ideas, small, specialized firms or innovation intermediaries have a promising future because of their competitive advantage compared to internal R&D labs of large businesses. These small firms can fully adapt their strategy and organization to play the role of an intermediary in technology or idea markets. This competitive advantage is based on a business model that connects suppliers of ideas and technologies to technology users. Examples of such innovation service providers are InnoCentive, Ninesigma, BIG, InnovationXchange, Ocean Tomo, and YourEncore.[6]

An example comes from a highly unusual venture capital firm, In-Q-Tel, which was created and funded by the U.S. Central Intelligence Agency. The CIA chose to create a new venture capital firm to give the intelligence community greater awareness of and access to the innovations of start-up firms in important areas like software and cryptography. Start-ups in these areas had been advised by their investors to steer clear of the Pentagon and its infamously bureaucratic procurement procedures, which was depriving the military of promising new technologies emerging from the start-up community. In-Q-Tel provided an entirely different pathway for these start-ups' innovations to reach the government intelligence and military communities, a pathway that was much less bureaucratic and more attractive for them and their investors.

Computers and Structures

One company that exemplifies the innovative potential of a specialist services innovator is Computers and Structures, Inc. (CSI) of Berkeley, California. Syed Hasanain is executive vice president of this engineering services company, which has more than fifty employees, including more than twenty in China. Founded in 1975, the company is best known for its SAP 2000 software program that performs structural analyses of buildings, bridges, towers, and other large civil engineering projects. The company's tools have been used to design the 1,432-foot-tall Petronas Towers in Malaysia, Taiwan's 1,667-foot-high Taipei 101, the 2,717-foot-tall Burj Khalifa in the United Arab Emirates (currently the world's tallest building), the new Dallas Cowboys stadium, and the new Yankee Stadium.[7] "Most of the world's most significant structures built in recent years have been designed with our software," Hasanain proudly tells me.

What makes these tools so helpful is their ability to help architects and engineers design structures in software and test them for stability in the face of winds, earthquakes, and other forces. The software creates three-dimensional images and displays the stresses of, for instance, vehicle traffic, in a color-coordinated scheme, where the colors allow users to see quickly where structural problems may exist in the design long before it is built (and when it is much, much less expensive to correct). Red signifies weaknesses in the structure, and blue spots indicate solid support, for example. The software tools allow engineers to create what-if analyses, to see how designs will perform under various stresses. The maximum load able to be supported is calculated by the software.

The company estimates that it is the world leader in its specific niche, offering its products in more than one hundred countries. Back in 2004, Hasanain and his colleague, Ashraf Habibullah, the founder and president of CSI, found street vendors selling pirated versions of their software in Istanbul. Although it is a back-handed compliment to be sure, it shows how strong the company's influence is that pirates would trouble themselves to copy its software.

More recently, the company has been expanding its presence in Asia, where much new building activity is taking place. Its local contingent in China is translating the software into Chinese, so that civil engineers can employ this tool in building there. The company also has donated its software to some of the Indian Institutes of Technology, along with funding to assist in developing curricula to train civil engineers on its use.

The company understands the value of openness. It provides free copies of its software to major engineering schools throughout the world. It also makes a practice of donating its software, as well as engineering support, in response to disasters around the world. In Haiti, for example, CSI software is being used to design the buildings that will replace those that crumbled in the 2010 earthquake there; the same is being done in response to a recent major quake in Turkey.

This might seem like a counterintuitive strategy, since these donations might reduce the company's sales. But the benefits of openness can be impressive. In the Dominican Republic, for example, the government mandates the use and submission of drawings from CSI software as a standard requirement for all permitted high-rise buildings. As a result, every civil engineer in the Dominican Republic has been trained with CSI's software. The company estimates that it has a 95 percent share of all the buildings constructed there—not a bad result from giving away one's software.[8]

Lessons for Services Firms in Specialist Businesses

In specialist situations, there is a mismatch between the scale of R&D investment required and the market opportunity to reward those investments. As a result, developing technological innovations internally in large companies leads to a suboptimal return on these investments. Specialist firms can outperform the large firms if they disintegrate the value chains through more open technologies or business models to create economics that better match the size of the market. Architectural firms designing new buildings can create their own design tools, but these would be used only on the companies' own projects. A specialist like CSI can market its software for use for many architects who are designing a wide variety of structures. This higher-volume use allows the company to afford to invest in substantial revisions to its tool (SAP 2000 is on version 14 as of this writing, for example) beyond what any internal architectural firm could justify.

Another good example is specialized engineering firms in the petroleum industry. Companies like Foster-Wheeler are assigned the job of designing the next $10 billion petrochemical refinery because they work for most of the major oil companies and have experience they can deploy from one assignment to the next. Since major refineries are not built often, no one petrochemical firm can accumulate and maintain sufficient expertise to perform these highly technical tasks internally.[9]

As with the niche business, technical obsolescence is a critical risk that must be managed here. Failure to keep up to date on the latest technologies and applications could sink a promising specialist services firm. A second risk is that the firm's very focus and specialization forces its customers to perform the integration tasks necessary to insert the firm's offerings into its customers' business processes. In some mature markets, specialist service customers increasingly insist on forcing their suppliers to provide more complete solutions, which may require the specialist to develop or extend its capabilities. CSI has learned to put its own engineers in direct contact with the engineers at its customers. Their personnel must therefore not only be technically skilled but also have interpersonal communication skills. In enterprise software, avionics, and automotive markets, for example, customers are forcing their top-tier suppliers to become systems integrators, forcing highly focused firms further down the value chain and squeezing their ability to add value if they fail to develop or extend their skills.

The greater R&D intensity in the specialist segment does afford greater switching costs for customers, in contrast to the niche segment. But the chances of being overtaken by a novel technological approach remain significant.

Another important risk for specialist service firms is the departure of key staff. These people have in-depth knowledge and experience and often have had extensive dealings with key customers as well. Over time, they may develop a good reputation in their own right. Much of the value of specialist services firms lies in the heads of their key personnel, and if they are not managed well, these people likely have alternatives beyond staying with the firm. As we saw in the previous chapter, the network of former GE aircraft engine mechanics became a significant competitor to GE for the aftermarket sales and service of its engines—one factor that prompted GE to offer the Power by the Hour program.

Employee satisfaction and retention become critical metrics to manage for companies that wish to sustain themselves as specialists. CSI, for example, has never lost anyone from the firm. One of its workers, a former professor from Johns Hopkins University, has been at CSI for more than twenty years. Hasanain himself has been with the company since he joined in 1989. It is common for many small specialist firms to create opportunities for such key personnel to become part-owners of the business, another way to keep them engaged.

In CSI's case, founder Ashraf Habibullah regards his coworkers "as part of my family." CSI never hires anyone unless he or she is recommended, and it relies strongly on referrals from current employees and others well known to the company. CSI's hiring is somewhat like an arranged marriage, since the backgrounds of both the company and the prospective employee are well known to both sides. To date, this careful hiring approach appears to be working well.

DOMINANT SERVICES BUSINESSES

Over time, very large markets promote greater specialization and usher in very large economies of scale in R&D. These are dominant businesses in Figure 7.2. Dominant businesses are the land of the giants, where smaller firms fear to tread unless they have made the investments necessary to achieve those economies of scale themselves. Smaller firms here usually must partner with large businesses in order to participate. Service innovation opportunities in this quadrant operate differently from the others in the matrix, because of the strength of the dominant large company partner.

MTV Networks

MTV Networks is one service business that was quite innovative initially and grew very large, very quickly as a result. Launched in 1981 by Robert Pittman, then an executive at Warner Cable, it pioneered a format that became known as music videos. The content for these videos was developed by independent artists and producers to be shown on MTV. The Buggles song "Video Killed the Radio Star" was, with intentional irony, the first video played on the network's first transmission.[10] It was clear from early on in its life that MTV Networks was going to be a national phenomenon, and the business quickly broke out of its initial niche and became part of the larger modern culture. But the business model was decidedly familiar to radio: create an audience of viewers and sell advertising to them. In this model, big advertisers develop a campaign with their own communication bureau, and it is placed through a media bureau with

TV stations as commercials. MTV simply became another media buy for companies trying to communicate with potential customers.

As the network became successful, it was sold off. Viacom acquired the network as part of its acquisition of Warner Cable. Over the years, the format for music television oscillated between periods of more music and periods of more reality TV shows and other nonmusic programming. By 2002, the category of music videos was widely established, along with reality TV shows that portrayed houses of strangers living together, or, in one show, the Ozzy Osbourne family.

In 2002, MTV Networks switched to another business model. Central to this model was the idea that advertisers were no longer seen as clients, but as partners in the creation of the concepts and content of the programming—a form of co-creation. Communication concepts now were jointly developed collectively for a specific target group, typically one or more kinds of young people—for example, college bound or working class, urban or rural, and from different geographical locales. To this end, MTV Networks has developed itself into an expert on youth culture.

The shows are no longer limited to being vehicles for advertising. Reality TV shows now provide a powerful opportunity for product placement for the client-partners' products as well. The most important difference from the previous business model is that risk and revenue sharing take place between MTV Networks and the advertisers, which essentially now co-create the programming content.

Lessons for Services Firms in Dominant Businesses

The most critical concerns in the dominant business area relate to sustaining a profitable business model over time and maintaining competitive differentiation from others over time. MTV's format—both the initial video broadcasting and the later reality TV shows—was rapidly copied. The company needs to keep innovating its format to stay ahead, and not all of the innovations have succeeded.

There is also the need for openness, even for large service companies. MTV got its initial programming from a loose network of bands, directors, record label promoters, and occasionally individuals. It remains collaborative today, working quite closely now with its advertisers, a marked change from its earlier broadcast model in developing content. Sustaining these collaborations over time is also challenging. The agendas of collaborating firms may coincide for some period of time, but they are likely to drift out of alignment eventually. One important way to increase the chances of sustaining collaboration is to be sure that the business models of the collaborators are aligned with each other.

Once these initial hurdles are passed, the collaborations must be managed so that they deliver on their potential. Slowinski and Segal put forward a three-stage model of collaboration management that involved executive sponsorship, relationship management, and project management, on both sides of the collaboration, as a means to manage collaboration.[11]

Another challenge in the dominant business is that large companies that team up with technologically savvy smaller firms often acquire or spin-in the latter when the technology becomes crucial in the further development of the business. Spin-ins or acquisitions are not necessarily problematic, since many technologies find their way to the market in this way and entrepreneurs are financially rewarded. However, integrating smaller services firms in large firms is a serious management challenge when the knowledge of founder or key employees plays a crucial role in the further development and commercialization of a product. If the firm is not alert and farsighted, the very talent it sought to acquire will leave the company immediately after the close of the transaction, leaving the dominant firm with a pale shadow of the value it had hoped to obtain.

Large companies also are learning that it might be more profitable to become a platform to attract a variety of smaller firms for collaboration rather than simply try to partner with or acquire a single firm. The advantage of platforms is that a network of small firms remains entrepreneurial and creative and can make quick decisions, while profiting from leveraging the tangible and intangible assets of the large firm. A second advantage is that they sometimes discover exciting opportunities that the large company did not know about. Yet through providing the platform for the small company to exploit the opportunity, the large firm benefits as well.[12]

THE ADVANTAGES OF OPEN INNOVATION FOR SMALLER SERVICE FIRMS

Services innovation is certainly important for large firms, but is also quite interesting for smaller firms in a world of open innovation. What is perhaps more interesting is the increasing number of opportunities for collaboration between large and small companies.[13] Large companies increasingly are interested in collaborative innovation partnerships with smaller firms because a smaller firm's expertise and focus can accelerate the completion time for a larger firm's innovation initiative.

There are also advantages of flexibility and deferred investment for the large firm. The large firm can leverage its considerable assets, such as its brand and its distribution system, without having to commit large amounts of fixed capital in advance. This lightens the balance sheet, increasing the firm's return on its financial assets. Meanwhile, the smaller firm now has access through its collaboration to brands and distribution channels that otherwise would have been prohibitively expensive to develop on its own.

Collaboration is also critical for building platforms. A smaller firm might find a services market to be an attractive size for it when that size would be too small to interest a large firm, so they move to join a prospective platform while it is still in the early stages of growth. Some large firms provide extensive technical information, comarketing opportunities, and even occasional subsidies for smaller firms' R&D costs in hopes of attracting them into offering services that support the large firm's platform.[14]

Other important service innovations sometimes come directly from users. These users can form companies themselves or become a starting point for another firm to develop new services offerings or enhancements that improve the quality or capability of a technology.[15] Many large companies are eager to encourage contributions from these users and foster the creation of open innovation communities. It may even serve the purposes of large firms better to allow the smaller firms to be seen as the leaders of these communities.

Open innovation fundamentally is about the greater intrusion of markets into the processes of innovation. SMEs have a greater ability to specialize than larger firms, and this specialization is more helpful precisely when markets are more available for innovative activities. Internally organized activities are restricted to a single captive customer operating in a single captive market. Open innovation activities seek to cultivate multiple customers in multiple markets for that innovative activity, spreading costs and risks of adoption more widely, and identifying new and exciting service applications that the single company operating in a single market might have missed. This creates significant business opportunities for smaller firms.

Innovation often happens first at the edge of markets rather than at the center of existing markets, and this is the great source of opportunity for smaller firms in the open innovation landscape. Smaller firms can participate sooner, move faster, and adapt more readily to opportunities that emerge from the periphery of a market relative to large firms. Which path makes the most sense for which smaller firms requires a careful assessment of R&D requirements and market opportunities. Clearly, there is no single answer; one size will not fit all SMEs.

Smaller firms have many different, important roles to play in services innovation. They can be explorers, pursuing markets that are too small (at least for now) to be of interest to large firms. They can be specialists, providing technological expertise to a variety of firms in a market that cannot support large firms. They can break out into large and growing markets, especially when the R&D investment is not overwhelming at the outset and their business model is truly innovative. They can partner with and support the dominant businesses and platforms of large firms. And they can remain in a niche, where large companies have no interest and pose no threat.

Smaller firms face many challenges in trying to compete in markets with large firms, yet they enjoy some unique advantages over those large firms, and so should not fear that competition. As long as they remain alert, adaptive, and focused, they can do well. Large firms would do well to orient themselves more externally to work with these firms. Smaller firms are potential suppliers, partners, or customers for large firms. Importantly, they often embody important innovation experiments in technologies or business models, experiments that could teach a great deal to observant large firms. And as the data in Figure 7.1 show, there is too much R&D activity in smaller firms for even the largest, most successful companies to ignore. We predict a healthy future for these smaller firms in the innovation systems of advanced economies.

o   o   o

The next chapter considers how services businesses themselves can innovate more effectively. In particular, services businesses must find ways to scale their businesses without losing the ability to give customers what they want.

CHAPTER 8

OPEN SERVICES INNOVATION FOR SERVICES BUSINESSES

Much of the discussion in this book so far has shown that businesses need to think of themselves as service businesses in order to escape the commoditization trap. Being a service business, however, is by no means enough to guarantee any organization an innovative future. You will need to build a platform for your services business, and sustaining it over time will require the platform to evolve so that it grows in value for your customers and others who participate in it. If you can do this, that platform can also grow in value for you as well.

We start with ways for your service to learn more from your customers and to do a better job of collecting information from your customers' use of your services. Then we see how to construct a platform with this knowledge, and finally create a platform that evolves over time for you and your allies, supporters, and partners in the platform.

GETTING SMARTER ABOUT YOUR CUSTOMERS

The marketing field has developed a number of techniques for companies to learn about their customers, including different kinds of market research. For example, customers who have purchased a particular product are invited to answer questions about it on a survey. In focus groups, customers are invited into a special room with a moderator to discuss their experiences with the product. Customer support specialists often ask customers specific questions about the product during or after a service inquiry. And there are many other mechanisms as well.

Although these approaches are time-tested, they all feature an element of unreality or a fabricated reality in their methodology:

- The customer is probed or engaged outside his or her normal context and consumer behavior process.
- The customer is interrupted by phone or by computer to reply to questions on a survey.
- The customer is brought into a focus group facility to discuss his or her opinions.
- The customer who calls the support line for help (and then is asked questions) is not doing his or her task but had to break away to contact customer support.

Many of these information-intensive services can be supplemented with new research techniques that collect data from customers in the course of their normal work activity. Note that there are important privacy issues to clear with customers in this process, but once they have given you permission to watch and learn from them, this is a far more authentic way to observe their behavior. Instead of interrupting your customers, you can now simply follow them in what anthropologists would call their "native habitat."

Knowing what your customers are using with your service gives you a far broader picture of the context of those customers. You may see unstated customer needs and opportunities to link items together, or consolidate them into a new, simpler device, or perhaps a service or suite of services that makes the items work better. Take the example of a home entertainment system. Many homes now host numerous devices: a TV (or more than one), a cable or satellite service, a VCR, a DVD player, a stereo hi-fi with separate speakers, and a video recorder such as TiVo or DVR.

Given this wide array of hardware and software, what do people actually watch? One of the most commonly accessed channels is the program listing channel, which is one of the slowest and least efficient ways imaginable to find interesting programs to watch—a clear opportunity for a new service. Such a service would add significant value to the rest of the system, since people care most about what programs they can view or record to watch later. What if a service provider could accurately recommend what a customer will want to watch based on his or her behavior, like Amazon does? The result would likely be higher customer satisfaction and more programs watched, with more advertising revenues received. The only cost would be learning a new way to access available programs rather than turning to the program listing channel.

CONSTRUCTING A PLATFORM FROM YOUR CUSTOMERS' EXPERIENCES

The new services insight is to observe customers in their environment, not yours, from an anthropological or behavioral point of view. Instead of imposing your own judgments or preferences on their behavior, these points of view strive to uncover how the customer is thinking, and identify the customer's own judgments or preferences. Once you have done this, you are in a position to create a platform and then improve it to meet customer needs even better.

Directly Observing Customers

One company that takes the importance of customer-driven services innovation to heart is Intuit, the personal financial software company. Intuit makes it a required process for employees, with the customer's permission, to follow customers home or to their office after purchasing an Intuit product. Once at the home or office, the Intuit employee closely observes the customer try to unwrap, install, and use the product and takes careful notes:

- What information does the customer use?
- What information does the customer ignore?
- Where in the process of installation does the customer encounter difficulties?
- What else is the customer using that interacts with the Intuit product?

- When the customer starts to use the product, what is the first activity that he or she performs?
- How long does all this take, from the time the package is unwrapped to the first successful performance of an activity?

The Intuit person is not there to make the problems go away for that customer, as a traditional customer service representative might do. Instead, the observer is there to identify any problems that arise and understand the context in which Intuit's product is being used. This information can be of great value in designing changes that increase every customer's success with the product in the future. It can also identify possible additional products or services that the company could offer.

One Intuit insight was that customers had to make many laborious entries from their credit card statements into Quicken, its checkbook program, to develop their household budget and track their spending. Intuit figured out how to automate this for customers. Later it offered a credit card that would record this automatically. When the company saw that some of its customers were using Quicken to run their small business, it created a new product, QuickBooks, to provide more capabilities to serve the needs of small businesses. A new growth business was born. The platform of offerings from Intuit expanded, and the company found new sources of revenue.

Another service provider that has achieved significant business success in a competitive market is the Geek Squad, part of Best Buy. This organization is known for its trademark 1960s-era geek outfits, complete with the black and white Volkswagens that they drive to their customers. The Geek Squad plays an important role in Best Buy's struggle against competitors, including behemoths like Walmart. When a customer buys a big screen TV, for example, Best Buy may not be able to beat Walmart's prices, but its Geek Squad, which charges for its services, provides Best Buy with the ability to get the customer's TV installed properly and in a short period of time, whereas the Walmart customer must install it himself or arrange for a third party to assist in the installation. With an extended warranty or additional items to complete the installation, the

Geek Squad provides additional high-margin revenues to what otherwise would be a commodity purchase. This is another example of economies of scope, where a customer can get many needs fulfilled by one provider or business.

Other ways to closely observe include taking a video of customers as they engage with a product or service. The video has the added advantage that others who could not be present can directly observe the customer's actions rather than read a report about them. Such direct evidence can be helpful in convincing others about the value of offering a new service. In building the service blueprints that we first saw back in Chapter Three, for example, video can be a powerful way to document the customer's experience with your service as it currently exists. You could take a video of a customer entering a restaurant and follow that customer throughout the meal, recording his or her interactions with the wait staff, other servers, other patrons, and other parts of the facility, including the parking. With everyone seeing the same video, discussions can move from arguments over what is currently provided to the service one wishes to provide instead.

Online Observation of Customers

In the online world, you don't have to be physically present to observe customers. You have access to enormous data streams, including the Web page where customers were prior to coming to your site and the page they go to when they leave your site. While they are on your site, you can easily collect data on which pages they go to (and which pages they don't) and how long they stay on each page. These customer patterns can point the way to new service offerings, bundled with other partners or offered by your own organization. They help uncover ways to assist customers with one-stop shopping and offer economies of scope to you.

There are a variety of ways to do this, and a discipline around this approach to learning from customers is growing.[1] One recent approach is to use semantic search techniques on user-generated content to uncover customers' own direct accounts of their experiences with products and services. NetBase in Mountain View, California, a company we met in

Chapter Seven, offers such a service. Working with customers, NetBase probes customer entries on Twitter, various blogs, Facebook, and other areas where a company's product or service is being discussed.

This approach offers important benefits. For one, the customer is in his or her own (online) environment, not yours. For another, you collect the customer's account of the experience in the customer's own language, with no interpretation or translation between you and the customer. A third benefit is that this approach can detect both positive and negative experiences early on. When a few customers write about something on a blog, usually a very small number of people read it. This gives more time for the company to recognize the opportunity or problem, and then take action to exploit it or address it. Unfortunately, many companies become aware of a problem only when it has reached the mass media, so that a large number of people have already learned about the problem before the company has taken notice of it. Services like those of NetBase provide an early warning system that can help companies get ahead of the mass media and learn about problems much sooner, possibly developing solutions as well as new services.

BUILDING A PLATFORM OUT OF YOUR SERVICES

Learning more about your customers before your competitors do is an effective way to improve your services. However, this is not enough to stay ahead. Over time, your competitors will learn by watching what services you provide and how you provide them. They can talk to your customers and your suppliers to learn more about you. They can hire away some of your people and gain inside knowledge of your workings and activities. Even when they don't know why you provide those services, they can imitate your offerings and draw customers away from you. Never underestimate the ability of competitors to learn from you.

For these reasons, it is not safe to rely only on excellent service to sustain your competitive advantage as a services provider. A more robust approach is to turn your service into a platform for others to build on. If you can successfully do this, you will attract others to work with your services. Some will use them in their own offerings, and others will build on them and extend your services into new areas. Partners will complement your services with their offerings, making yours more valuable in the process. And even individuals can add to the richness, variety, and quality of your services if you succeed in crafting the platform that invites them to do so.

Some of the actions you will need to pull this off have already been discussed in this book, but it is worth reviewing them here. One set of actions is to share valuable information with suppliers and customers that helps them get more out of your service. It is common for retailers, for example, to provide suppliers with extensive information about the retailer's sales of their products. In some cases, retailers let the supplier manage the portion of shelf space in the retail store that the retailer has set aside for the supplier. This takes costs out of the supply chain for the retailer and makes the supplier more efficient. The retailer may even sell this information to the supplier. In this case, the retailer has a platform with a service providing sales analytics to suppliers.

Another set of actions is to invite customers to co-create service experiences with you. Giving customers access to parts of your service and letting them tell you what they want and how often they want it can build customer loyalty and satisfaction. Watching what customers do and learning what they would like to be able to do can point you to further improvements and even new markets for your services. One area where this has worked well is with the German software company SAP and its developer network. SAP used to manage relations with this group quite closely, restricting access and carefully controlling what information was provided to their developers. But SAP leaders have more recently learned that it helps their business to facilitate developers' talking directly to one another. Developers encounter similar challenges in building applications and services for SAP, and they can help each other solve these problems more rapidly (and with very high quality) than they can if SAP must provide every answer to every question. SAP has created a platform for developers to share information about SAP.

SAP has taken this one step further by giving developers who have questions the ability to award points to developers who provide answers to these questions. SAP keeps track of the points, which become a currency (developer points) that it controls and allows talented developers to build their reputation within this community by receiving lots of these developer points. Many now put their SAP points on their résumé as evidence to prospective employers of their skills within the SAP community. This is an innovative way to motivate openness.

Another way to build services into a platform is to create a certification program that trains capable, interested third parties in how to use your services effectively. Microsoft has more than seventy thousand independent software vendors that it has certified. It then sorts these certified vendors into silver, gold, and platinum levels, so that users of Microsoft-certified services can differentiate the levels of skills among these third parties. Being a Platinum Microsoft developer requires significant investments by the third party in training and skill development. These investments create greater loyalty by those Platinum partners as a result and a nice business for Microsoft.

AMAZON: A PLATFORM LEADER THAT IS STILL EVOLVING

Amazon is an exemplar of a services provider that has truly innovated its offerings. In fact, it has applied many of the concepts in this book successfully and built an outstanding and profitable platform that continues to evolve to this day.[2]

Amazon began life as an online book seller, a business that remains an important part of its revenues. It would be a much less important company today if it had contented itself with just selling books. Its business activities today involve selling an increasingly wide variety of items, even to the point of reselling its own capabilities as an online retailer, using its Web sites and servers as platforms. Amazon also resells its infrastructure to other companies to use for hosting their Internet activities. Now it is creating device platforms like its Kindle, complete with e-books and other media, and attractive pricing to stimulate purchase of it.

Amazon was formed in 1994 by Jeff Bezos in Seattle, Washington. At that time, he wanted to be among the first to use the nascent Internet as a medium for selling things. He chose books as his initial focus (the term *Amazon* was inspired by the deep wealth of items on his Web site, like the deep recesses of the world's largest jungle). Its 1995 opening claimed that it was "Earth's Biggest Bookstore," a grand claim for a tiny start-up company. It remained focused on that business through its initial public offering in 1997 and into 1998. This focus enabled the company to build increasingly capable internal processes for processing orders in its computer order entry systems (the customer did the order entry for the company, a huge savings over more traditional book delivery methods) and for shipping high volumes of merchandise.

There was a very attractive business aspect to this. Amazon received the customer's order and the customer's money at the beginning of its process. Like Dell Computer, Amazon had a positive cash flow as a result, since it incurred its costs of filling the order only after the cash was in hand. This allowed it to finance much of its growth directly from its customers, and what seemed like slim margins to many became more attractive once the cash flows were factored in.

Once these processes were up and running and beginning to achieve significant economies of scale, Amazon began looking for new sources of growth. Bezos and his team decided to add music CDs and videos to the business in 1998. In 1999, toys, electronics, tools, and software were added to the site. In 2000, cell phones, kitchen products, and lawn and patio products joined the site. These additions helped to deliver economies of scope for the company, attracting more buyers and giving all buyers more reasons to buy there. Although many of these items were bulkier and more expensive to ship than the original books, Amazon retained a core element of its business model: its ability to get its cash in advance from customers before incurring expenses to fulfill the order. A second element of Amazon's model, its customer acquisition, became more and more valuable as the company boosted the variety and range of products it could sell into a growing customer base. Amazon was becoming a significant platform through which multiple suppliers could reach consumers.

Investing in the Platform

Building the capabilities to take in millions of orders from millions of customers for hundreds of thousands of items, then obtain the merchandise, and then ship it on to the customer was not cheap. Sophisticated inventory management, fulfillment, and managing product information are expensive. In 2002, Bezos estimated that he had spent more than $800 million in his computer infrastructure to handle all of these activities.[3] At the time, some analysts criticized Amazon for overspending on its infrastructure. They thought of Amazon as a retailer, but Amazon saw itself differently. It saw a potential future as a provider of a wide range of products and services, and this large investment was a necessary step on the road to get there. Amazon aspired to be a platform.

Amazon also was quick to figure out ways to let its customers co-create with them. Amazon prominently featured reviews written by readers on its site. It listed the sales rank of the books that it sold for all to see. Amazon had even figured out how to employ collaborative filtering, whereby it could show site visitors that "60 percent of the people who bought X also bought Y." This was a clever way to employ technology to solve an increasingly important problem: When there is so much to choose from, how does a buyer know what to choose? And notice that Amazon's ability to reflect the choices of its past customers to its next customers grows better and better as more customers do more transactions with Amazon. As Jim Spohrer of IBM's Almaden Labs said to me, "Having recommendations of what a few hundred other people bought isn't very useful to me. Having recommendations based on what millions of other people have purchased, now that is very useful." So Amazon's business model becomes more valuable as its transactions increase in number.

Opening Up the Platform

As a leading online retailer, Bezos could have chosen to continue to build out Amazon's own selection of merchandise to offer to its customers. This would have been quite consistent with the closed innovation paradigm, where in order to deliver an extraordinary experience to customers, one performs all the necessary tasks oneself. However, Amazon went in a different direction. It decided to open up its powerful online reselling Web site to other merchants for them to list their own merchandise. This openness unleashed powerful economies of scope for the company, attracting hundreds of other suppliers to Amazon as a place to sell their own wares, a platform for reselling.

This has not been an easy process for Amazon. In 1999, the company initiated its zShops program with third-party merchants whereby these merchants were given a separate part of the Amazon site to display their own wares. Amazon initially let the merchants handle the purchase and fulfillment of these items. But customer complaints led Amazon to gradually take over more and more of the payment piece from the merchants. Later Amazon even took over the display and merchandising of the third-party merchants. These external merchants' items now have access to the same product pages on the Amazon Web site as Amazon's own merchandise. Today if a customer orders a piece of jewelry from Amazon, a third party actually fulfills the order. However, the Amazon customer might never realize that the order came from outside Amazon (unless there is a problem with the order or unless the customer wants to get Prime Free Shipping and finds that it doesn't apply).

The drive to more openness continued. Amazon began to partner with large retailers that wanted their own Web site to offer merchandise. They realized that Amazon knew a lot about running a retail Web site, and wanted to hire that experience and put it to work for themselves. Amazon could have treated its expertise in this area as a trade secret and refused to offer its knowledge to others. Instead, Amazon saw a new business opportunity to create more value from its knowledge of Internet retailing. It helped third-party retailers develop their own Web sites and then went further. Amazon hosted these third-party sites for such retailers on its own servers, becoming their infrastructure supplier. In some cases, Amazon even performed the merchandising and fulfillment portions of the transaction for the retailer. This was a more leveraged way for Amazon to get paid for its knowledge.

More recently, Amazon has created yet another business that exploits its knowledge. It offers its Elastic Cloud Computing Services to potential customers. Many companies that are much smaller than Amazon lack the volume of business and the expertise to develop and manage their own IT equipment and people. Amazon offers these companies the possibility of letting Amazon do that work for them. Amazon will host a company's IT functions and charge only for those services actually consumed. For customers, what was a large fixed investment in an area where they lacked much relevant expertise was converted to a variable expense managed by someone far more experienced and knowledgeable.

Lessons from Amazon for Open Services Innovation

Amazon's growing number of businesses nicely illustrates some of the points noted in this book about new ways to think about services innovation. Amazon's extensive partnering with third-party merchants, combined with its own relentless expansion into new categories of merchandise, create tremendous economies of scope for the company. Visitors to Amazon can increasingly shop for a wide variety of their needs—a one-stop-shopping experience that many customers value. And that experience is quite consistent across the site: ordering books is very much like ordering jewelry or garden tools or toys or electronics. This exemplifies the value of economies of scope for Amazon's customers.

Hosting other retailers' Web sites and offering its Elastic Cloud Computing Services demonstrate the value businesses can realize from harnessing economies of scale. By augmenting its own extensive transactions with those transactions of third parties, Amazon's infrastructure gets used more and more. Although this infrastructure has very high fixed costs to establish, the marginal costs of using the infrastructure are quite minimal. The key is to use the infrastructure at a high level of frequency. Amazon gets the best prices on IT equipment among all Internet retailers. It knows the best locations for server farms and can attract and keep the best IT management talent. And the more activity Amazon attracts, the more these advantages grow for it.

This is why Amazon can make a healthy margin on its infrastructure while providing a very good deal for its customers of that infrastructure. Infrastructure customers save themselves the fixed costs of purchasing, installing, operating, servicing, and maintaining the infrastructure. For them, these services become variable costs instead of fixed costs. For Amazon, these services add volume to their utilization, and Amazon's skills at running IT infrastructure are world class—far better than most of its infrastructure customers could hope to achieve on their own. More subtly, it raises the bar for any would-be competitors that wish to take away Amazon's third-party hosting business, or achieve the same costs as Amazon in online retailing. Any would-be competitor would have to reach Amazon's volume of transactions to develop the capabilities to perform these functions at a level comparable to Amazon itself. A few companies, such as Google, Microsoft, and IBM, have taken up the challenge. Traditional Amazon competitors like Barnes & Noble or Borders have not.

Amazon has hit on a formula for escaping the commodity trap. Its formula does not lie in the individual elements of its model. Others have copied the idea of retailing goods through the Internet. Others are selling books online. Many offer advice on what to buy based on what others have previously purchased. And now other companies are offering to rent their IT infrastructure to customers. Rather, Amazon's formula is powerful and sustainable because of how it puts the pieces together and how often it puts those pieces together. It leverages its tremendous volume of retailing activity to generate significant economies of scope for its customers. No other online retail site can match the scope of its offerings. This gives Amazon more knowledge about more customers than any other online or bricks-and-mortar retailer—an advantage that will last indefinitely. Amazon also processes an enormous number of transactions, making it one of the most efficient transactions-processing companies in the world. This gives it enormous economies of scale that only a relative handful of other companies can match. And none of the latter have the retail presence that Amazon has.

Although Amazon undoubtedly will face continued challenges going forward, it appears to have a bright and prosperous future. It has built this future through the creation and growth of its service business, which has become a platform for Internet retailing. Its knowledge of its customers and its willingness to open its platform to others will be difficult for others to commoditize.

o o o

Many of Amazon's investments provide it worldwide opportunities for its services business. This raises the question of how Open Services Innovation applies outside the United States. In the next chapter, we consider this innovation in the context of emerging markets.

CHAPTER 9

OPEN SERVICES INNOVATION IN EMERGING ECONOMIES

To this point, we have examined the importance of services in advanced economies—those characterized by high living standards, high wages, and substantial specialization of labor. As we have seen, customers benefit from the ability to reduce their total cost of searching for, receiving, and consuming products through one-stop shopping. And services companies can deliver these benefits cost-effectively by developing economies of scale in their operations through standardizing many of their processes, and incorporating more knowledge about their customers' prior experiences.

The context in emerging economies differs in important ways from that of the advanced economies: living standards and wages are lower, there is less specialization of labor, and saving time for customers is of less immediate value to most of those customers. Even the ability to achieve economies of scale may be diminished if the infrastructure in the less developed country is unable to support it. Power generation may be uneven, transportation may be impaired, and water quality is not assured in these economies.

In this chapter, we consider the role of services innovation in the context of less developed countries. Although there are important differences with advanced economies, many of the points that we have seen in this book nevertheless remain highly relevant. Since it would be a mistake to try to characterize all developing economies as being the same, the chapter examines a few organizations operating in India and China. These are not intended to represent organizations in all developing economies (or even all of India or China). They are nevertheless illustrative of services innovation challenges and opportunities that can arise in developing economies. Examining these organizations here is useful for comparing their challenges and opportunities to those discussed already for advanced economies.

There is a further importance to this chapter. Most of the growth in the world economy for the foreseeable future is going to take place in emerging rather than the developed economies. So services innovators that are looking to grow must think globally but compete locally (that is, in the context of the emerging economies, where most of that growth will occur). This chapter provides some indicators for how services innovators can compete in the local environment.

That is not all. Indigenous innovators who are arising in the emerging economies may one day challenge services innovators in the developed world. They will not compete with the business models, overheads, and assumptions from the developed world but instead will adapt successful models forged in environments where costs have to be much lower.[1] The concern for innovators in the advanced economies is not that these models will be better in delivering services, but rather that they will be good enough to meet the needs of many. Then the innovators in emerging economies may be positioned to disrupt their rivals.[2] This chapter sketches some of the business models that successful services innovators have developed in India and China, models that one day could be adapted to enter into the United States, Japan, and Western Europe.

ASIAN PAINTS: OPEN SERVICES INNOVATION IN A TRADITIONAL PRODUCT INDUSTRY

Asian Paints sells a very traditional product: paint.[3] It has grown to become one of the largest and most successful paint companies in India and now is expanding its operations into Southeast Asia and the Middle East. Founded in India in 1942, the company had the strategic intent "to reach consumers in the remotest corners of the country" with paints.[4] Often these paints were packaged in small quantities as part of making the company's products affordable to villagers and to the many distribution channels used to reach those remote corners.

Today company sales exceed $1 billion. It operates twenty-eight plants, with eighteen processing centers, six regional distribution centers, and seventy-two depots.[5] Yet the company's mission statement bears a marked resemblance to that at its founding: "Going where the customer is."

This is not an easy task in India, a country with more than forty regional dialects and no single national language. Its infrastructure is underdeveloped, such that many towns and villages lack any paved roads to access them. In monsoon season, these areas can be difficult to reach. Social infrastructure is a work in process, and illiteracy remains an obstacle for many adults and children.

The Challenge of Commoditization

The paint industry in India offers a number of challenges. The country comprises numerous and quite diverse regions, and each has paint companies competing actively within it. Asian Paints is among the largest firms, but there are other large firms in the market. Foreign firms also are eyeing the market for entry, and the many smaller domestic competitors have kept prices low for everyone.

Suppliers had strengthened their bargaining power over the paint industry, creating additional business challenges. Petroleum manufacturers and chemicals companies have raised prices multiple times, squeezing margins for all of the paint suppliers. Rising demand in India (ordinarily a good thing for paint manufacturers) even coincided with occasional supply shortages, causing input prices to rise still further. And these prices never seemed to come down as quickly as they went up.

Distribution was also complex for Asian Paints. There were many potential channels for paints to reach the final consumer, and some of these overlapped. Many consumers did not use paint themselves but contracted with paint applicators or installers to paint their homes or buildings for them. The customer would choose a color or set of colors, and then the applicator would order the paint and paint the house as requested. The applicators typically chose where to buy the paint and what brand of paint to buy, so saving time was not very important for many customers. There were other purchase influencers, such as the applicators, who were important in choosing which paint to buy. Since most paints lacked a strong brand, there were few ways to fight against this commoditization.

To escape the pressures of commoditization, Asian Paints decided in the mid-1990s to position itself as a premium brand and thereby create a strong brand preference among applicators and discerning consumers.[6] It launched an ambitious and expensive campaign to create a positive brand image and updated its packaging for all of its paint products as well.

The brand campaign failed to inspire any consumer interest. It appeared that price was the primary purchasing criterion for most consumers in the paint market, which is emblematic of a commoditized market. Disappointed, the company went back to the drawing board. It seemed that traditional marketing techniques were not going to get it out of the commoditization trap.

Later in the 1990s, Asian Paints undertook a consumer research study aimed at understanding the perception of consumers about the product category as a whole. Asian Paints came to understand that its brand needed to be about people and homes to strengthen that emotional connection. So it launched a campaign that translated to, "Every home has a story to tell." The insight for Asian Paints was that this theme could be directly translated into paint, because "every color has a story to tell" inside the home.[7] The company began to make consumers care about paint by connecting it directly to things that consumers really did care about (festivals and home). This positioning went beyond advertising to include a new research partnership with the Indian Institutes of Technology to explore new colors and conduct research on colors. The company was beginning to use Open Innovation.[8]

Touching the Customer More Directly

As the campaign to differentiate itself began to build momentum, Asian Paints executives realized in 2001 that the firm's long-term growth depended on their ability to forge closer ties to their end consumers. Until that point, Asian Paints was typical of most manufacturers that dealt frequently with their direct customers: the distributors, resellers, and stock jobbers that stocked their products and sold them to the applicators and end customers. But Asian Paints had to rely on its direct contacts for information about end customer needs, shifts in needs, and preferences. Inevitably something was lost in the communication, so the company decided to invest in ways to reach out to end customers directly.

One source of direct contact became the customer help line, a service that allowed customers who had questions to contact Asian Paints directly for answers. This reduced the burden on Asian Paints' channel partners to deal with customer issues and complaints and introduced a direct line of contact for Asian Paints with end customers. From analyzing these calls, Asian Paints learned that its customers had unmet expectations when it came to service and overall project execution of painting projects. They lacked enough information to know what paints to buy, where to buy them, or how reputable a particular applicator or installer was to deal with. This kind of information was not commonly shared with Asian Paints by its direct customers. Like the children of Garrison Keillor's Lake Wobegon, all applicators described themselves as "above average."

From Customer Help to Services Innovation

The unmet needs that Asian Paints identified triggered an experiment that succeeded in providing another valuable way to differentiate itself. Asian Paints made the decision to move from a strictly product-based manufacturing business toward one that also incorporated a services model. Such a model would not only provide paint; it would also provide advice and information about which colors go best with other colors in their line of paints and offer designs for customers to follow. It would also help customers identify reputable installers and applicators. With the launch of Asian Paints Home Solutions, the firm would build a service brand by offering these value-added services, plus others ranging from in-person color recommendations to feng shui consultations.

Asian Paints hired outside designers to create new patterns and designs that could guide customers to choose particular combinations of paints and colors and to a network of qualified applicators who could, if desired, install that look in customers' homes. The goal was to deliver an Asian Paints signature look through the use of specific color combinations and themes, along with detailed application instructions to enable applicators and installers to deliver the desired result. This effort required Asian Paints not simply to answer the consumer help line but also to create a new, separate set of phone and online resources to field queries from channel partners and applicators about the Home Solutions offerings.

A Virtual Back Office for Channel Partners

The development of a list of recommended applicators could have alienated some of Asian Paint's traditional channel partners. However, another clever innovation that accompanied this new service offering was the ability of channel partners and applicators to obtain status information on each job (from quote, to a signed order, to receiving the paint, to completed job, to receiving final payment) they entered into Asian Paints Home Solutions system. This system became part of the channel's back office, recording status activities, outstanding jobs, new bids, and updates. For many channel partners, this was the first time their activities were computerized. So Asian Paints took care to include its distribution partners in the new initiative and provided added value to them as well as to end customers. This is another example of economies of scope but now in a new context: taking over more of the work of the distribution partners, who were the representatives of the company with the end consumer.[9]

This greatly improved the transparency of the entire solution offering for Asian Paints and its channel partners. The new solution would allow both the provider and Asian Paints Home Solutions to view all customer interactions and financial information in real time. This same system would also provide updates on the status of marketing rewards programs that were run by Asian Paints from time to time. In addition, the service allowed solution providers to generate a variety of sales, leads, and activity analysis reports. This functionality could even tabulate results of the customer surveys submitted at the completion of a job. In general, this system greatly increased the amount of information most solution providers had about their customers and their business. It also revealed project and consumer information to Asian Paints for the first time, a key strategic benefit from this initiative.

With vastly better data, Asian Paints was able to implement changes to take cost and time out of its processes with its many channel partners. The company was able to greatly improve its ability to forecast orders and volumes in this segment. This streamlined inventories, recovering working capital often tied up in transit in the old system. It also improved the response time between when a new job was entered and an order received and when that order could be fulfilled. The percentage of time when the required paint was not available was also greatly reduced.

Although there were challenges and bumps in the road as the Home Solutions offering was implemented, the results of the initiative were encouraging. In the first phase of the program, Asian Paints served more than 34,000 installations. In the four years after the implementation went live, 17,500 persons registered for Asian Paints Home Solutions consultations, and of these, 5,000 signed up for painting jobs. Revenues grew rapidly, amounting to nearly $10 million in fiscal year 2007—a doubling of revenue from the program in just three years. Margins, though not publicly revealed, were reported to be attractive as well.

Strong secondary benefits were realized from the project as well. The new solution gives Asian Paints greater visibility into all of its end customer interactions. As a result, the company has gained a deeper understanding of the needs of its end customers and has been able to modify its service business to better meet these needs. Asian Paints also has reduced the time it takes to attract a new customer and convert that customer into a user of its products. Nearly 25 percent of its Home Solutions business is coming from referrals from satisfied customers, and about 7 percent so far has been from repeat business by current customers.[10]

Using Services Innovation to Escape the Commoditization Pressure

Competitors now confront a new Asian Paints. Previously they could entice distributors, dealers, and applicators to switch to their paint from

Asian Paints, perhaps by offering a discount, or a rebate, or free samples. These price-based methods were effective in the product-focused commodity business that Asian Paints confronted in the 1990s. It kept margins low, and Asian Paints often had to match discounts or rebates to keep its business.

As Asian Paints implements its Home Solutions network, however, it is raising the bar for what competitors must do to lure its customers away. Being out of stock is expensive for distributors and dealers. Waiting for the proper paint causes downtime for applicators, which is very expensive for them. Not having the designs that consumers are asking for and not being able to answer questions from consumers when they want to know more about how a design will look can lose the entire business to a competitor. The new Asian Paints approach takes total costs down in the system, while allowing the company to claim a greater share of value for itself. The approach is boosting its margins while still allowing its channel partners to enjoy better service and lower costs.

Competitors essentially must create their own services network if they are to compete effectively with that of Asian Paints. This will not be easy for them, as it was not easy for Asian Paints. The smaller companies lack the scale and scope of offerings to do this economically. The larger companies must transform their business processes substantially in order to pull it off. They will need to become coordinators in the network and actively manage this transformation.[11] And execution matters. Early errors from poor implementation can spoil the word-of-mouth that a services innovation transformation initiative needs in order to build momentum both within the company and the market. Asian Paints has a sizable head start on the rest of the industry.

In 2002, and again in 2003, *Forbes* magazine rated Asian Paints one of the best small companies in the world. The company now is selling its products in more than twenty-one countries around the globe and is rapidly becoming a rather large company. Having mastered distribution in this complex country, Asian Paints is well positioned to tackle the challenges of marketing and distribution in its newer markets: the Persian Gulf, Malaysia, Vietnam, and China. As it does so, it will again need to focus not only on the end customer but the many disparate distribution and influencer channels that guide consumer choices in these markets. It will need to employ services innovation again to drive business to itself in the commoditizing paint industry.

SHANGHAI SILICON IP EXCHANGE

Shanghai Silicon IP Exchange (SSIPEX) is one of three centers created in China to facilitate the legal exchange of semiconductor intellectual property (IP). As such, it is a service provider that acts as a source of information for new semiconductor technology and serves two purposes: a distribution channel for semiconductor technology owners and a demonstration center for local customers who come to SSIPEX to learn about the latest technology developments and assess which, if any, would be suitable for them to use in their next product.

SSIPEX focuses on collecting, evaluating, and disseminating the technologies that bridge between the design of a new chip and the foundry process that makes the chip. It operates by working with owners of semiconductor technology to accumulate libraries of manufacturing design tools, reference designs, and other useful knowledge. It then invites local Chinese companies to try this technology. If the Chinese company finds the technology useful, SSIPEX helps to broker a license of the IP to the Chinese company. About 70 percent of the IP at SSIPEX comes from outside China and 30 percent from within the country. It currently boasts more than three thousand individual pieces of semiconductor IP, making it the second largest commercial repository of its kind in the world. Unlike the repositories of private foundry firms (such as SMIC, the largest foundry in China, or Taiwan Semiconductor Manufacturing Corporation, which we met in Chapter Two), SSIPEX is open to all members, regardless of which foundry members choose to use for building their designs.

SSIPEX is part of a larger network of centers to demonstrate and legally transfer semiconductor-related IP. A sister center, ICC, focuses on providing legal access for Chinese companies to design services platforms in semiconductors, such as electronic design automation tools. Another sister organization, ICRD, focuses on providing Chinese firms with authorized access to manufacturing process platforms to help them build the designs they develop. The SSIPEX Center, built in 2003, was funded by the Shanghai city government with 30 million RMB funding and the national government's Ministry of Industry and Information with 10 million funding RMB (this combined funding amounted to about $5 million).

SSIPEX's revenue comes from three sources: a membership fee charged to companies that want access to the IP, a fee charged to IP owners who want to display their IP, and transaction fees for brokerage transactions between the members and the IP owners. Although the first two sources have been the dominant sources of revenue to date, SSIPEX expects the third source to grow as more Chinese companies learn about their services and understand how to use them.

Although SSIPEX is very young, it is beginning to make investments to add more value to its member companies as they sample the different tools on offer in the extensive library of IP at the Exchange. The company now employs a handful of consultants and analysts to assist member companies. An investment in 2006 established a laboratory inside SSIPEX. This laboratory functions as a black box, such that customers can bring a sample of their design to the lab, and the lab will produce a partial layout (or other output, depending on the specific IP being tested). But the black box will prevent customers from seeing exactly how the output was obtained and will keep them from trying to reverse-engineer or otherwise appropriate the technology. The customer therefore gets more detailed information on the value of the technology he is trying to use, while the IP owner of the technology is protected from misappropriation.

The SSIPEX is an exciting experiment in innovative ways to facilitate the exchange of semiconductor technology. The organization nonetheless faces some daunting challenges. One problem is that SSIPEX's customers are small companies. In China, many people believe that because labor is cheap, it is more affordable to develop technology on their own. There is no appreciation among companies that leveraging external IP could save time and improve the quality of the resulting product. This mentality is widespread and will require extensive education before many companies will evaluate external technologies as part of their internal product development process.

Another infrastructure challenge is the underdeveloped legal system standing behind the legal protection of semiconductor technology. SSIPEX takes careful steps to ensure that the IP it offers is legally obtained. However, it does not have the resources to monitor the use of the IP by the small Chinese companies that are its customers. If the customers are illegally reselling or otherwise transferring the IP to others without proper authorization, SSIPEX might not know about it. And if it did detect such activity, it is unclear how effective any recourse would be to the Chinese courts.

As a service provider, SSIPEX might be able to avoid direct involvement and leave any legal actions to the IP owners whose rights were infringed. But if IP owners determine that SSIPEX is undermining their ownership position in China, it would damage the development of legal IP exchange in the Chinese semiconductor industry for everyone. Moreover, successful infringement actions might even diminish the willingness of SSIPEX members to consider external technologies, for fear of exposing themselves to such suits, even if they ultimately do not employ the technologies in their designs.

The lack of infrastructure, in this case a relatively transparent legal system and a body of case law showing how that system works in practice, is constraining this services provider as well.

SHAANGU: A PRODUCT-BASED COMPANY MOVES INTO SERVICES

The Shaan'Xi Blower Group Co. (which I refer to as ShaanGu) was founded in 1975 in the city of Xian, China. The company traditionally was a manufacturer of industrial products like turbo compressors and blowers.[12] Prior to 2001, it enjoyed a large market share in its domestic market in China, and its main business focused on the fabrication of a single product: an industrial blower. But the company raised its sights in

2001 and began to compare itself to outstanding foreign competitors like MAN Turbo and Siemens in Germany and Mitsui Co. in Japan.

Company leaders soon realized that these foreign competitors were using a different business model from the product-focused model that they had been following. Siemens and Mitsui made excellent (albeit expensive) products. Their offerings to customers went well beyond their product line, including services like technology development, technology consulting, technology service, financial services, engineering services, and even the complete design of plants for using their machinery. By providing a total solution for their clients, foreign firms were making a lot more money than ShaanGu was, and ShaanGu had great difficulty competing with them. Like many other firms in China, ShaanGu was winning business located at only the low end of the value chain. It had to win its business on the basis of price and rapid delivery (production capacity is constrained for these expensive items, making the ability to deliver more rapidly an advantage). This high degree of product focus, ShaanGu concluded, had high risks compared to the risks these foreign firms faced, not least because other Chinese companies could enter into the low end of the business as well.

Adopting an Open Services Innovation Focus

In 2001, ShaanGu decided to transform its strategy from a product-focused to a service-focused strategy. As a result of this decision, it launched a number of new services businesses:

o o o

• *Services to help clients install the product.* In addition to providing the host machine, ShaanGu is responsible for providing the complete equipment (including system design, system equipment supply, and installation and debugging) and engineering contract for its clients. Soon after this, ShaanGu provided clients with a further range of lifetime service solutions and options.

- *Servicing all of its products for clients once installed.* After outsourcing its low knowledge-intensive business of equipment maintenance to outside professional companies, ShaanGu reorganized its resources and professionals to engage in more profitable value-added maintenance and repair and overhaul service businesses. It developed process monitoring and fault diagnosis systems to provide overall process control and all-weather condition management services for its clients' equipment. It offered monitoring reports for clients periodically. By using remote accident-diagnosis and other professional systems, ShaanGu provides clients with more rapid, timely, and efficient professional maintenance and repair and overhaul services. From 2001 to 2004, ShaanGu's orders for maintenance, repair, and overhaul services increased 47 percent annually. The value of these orders rose above 100 million RMB, giving the services business new stature within the company.

- *Managing spare parts on behalf of clients.* As is typical for expensive capital equipment, spare parts costs over the useful life of the equipment can rise to as much as the initial acquisition cost for ShaanGu products. Customers who need spare parts can have difficulty finding them on short notice. Previously they had to use funds to reserve and store spare parts for later use, if and when they were needed. Naturally, not all of these reserved parts were eventually needed, and some of the needed parts hadn't been reserved in advance. To deal with this dilemma, ShaanGu began to set up spare parts depots and provide clients spare parts logistics services rapidly once the parts were needed. This reduced the downtime risk for operating the machines and reduced spare parts costs for clients. It also gave ShaanGu better data on actual breakdowns and spare parts use, a knowledge advantage that allowed it to optimize its own provision of parts and reduce its own costs for keeping its customers' machines up and running.

- *Assistance for customers with financing ShaanGu products.* Many of ShaanGu's customers were small or medium-sized enterprises in China. These customers often encountered loan difficulties because banks and financial institutions would limit the extension of credit to them to control credit risk. Not only did this impair the customers' ability to keep their production lines up and running with the best equipment, it also reduced the ability of ShaanGu to sell its equipment to these customers. By contrast, ShaanGu was a highly respected, reputable firm that enjoyed easy access to the credit markets due to its solid financial strength. ShaanGu realized that it could advance its business and learn more about its customers by providing financial options for equipment purchase for clients. This has proven to be a key factor in the success of ShaanGu's services business, even against its foreign competition. The recent financial troubles in the West have not hit Shaan'Xi province where ShaanGu is located nearly as much, so ShaanGu currently enjoys a relative advantage in the financial markets.

A New Business Model for ShaanGu

Based on this strategy transition, ShaanGu also transformed its business model from one that is product based to one that is service based. Before, the company made its money on whatever differentiation it could achieve in its industrial products. While that remains an important factor, the company now makes additional profits from the services it offers beyond the products themselves. This also lets the company become more flexible in bidding for business at new accounts, because it can mix and match its product and service offerings into bundles that best match the client's budget and requirements. And the company now learns a great deal more about its clients as a result of its services offerings. This allows it to improve the design of its future products to reduce common failure points; optimize the location, logistics, and provision of spare parts; and understand how clients will actually use the products (which in turn can inspire the design of innovative future products).

Initial Results

ShaanGu has been pleasantly surprised by the results of its transformation so far. The share of company revenue created by its services business continues to rise in comparison to its product sales. In 2005 an important milestone was reached when the services business accounted for more than half of total company sales (56 percent) for the first time. In 2009 its sales reached 8.4 billion RMB. More than 80 percent of sales in 2009 came from selling solutions that combined products and services.

Profits are also increasing. The profitability gap between ShaanGu and its top-ranked foreign competitors enterprise apparently has narrowed. For example, the return on equity capital of ShaanGu has gone from less than 1/20 of that of German MAN Turbo Co. in 2001 to a roughly equivalent level in 2009. These results show that ShaanGu is moving out of the low end of its market and into the higher end, more value-added-services portion of that market. It is becoming a more capable supplier to its customers as a result, and a more formidable competitor as well.

OPEN SERVICES INNOVATION IN EMERGING ECONOMIES

Lessons Learned

These examples in this chapter show many similarities with the themes of the earlier chapters, as well as some differences. First, let us return to the themes in this book and examine the cases in this chapter with regard to them. Table 9.1 summarizes this examination

The first theme is that of co-creating with one's customers as a key aspect of services innovation. ShaanGu is perhaps the clearest example here in which the company offers to work with customers to design the physical manufacturing facilities into which its equipment will then be installed. Asian Paints enables co-creation within its distribution system by hosting the projects for its distributors and applicators online and helping them select paints and designs for the end customer. SSIPEX is a broker that does not yet offer design consulting services to its clients (which then might enable co-creation activities). Design consulting services would be a natural extension of its current services, albeit one that would require additional technical capabilities from its staff.

A second theme is that of specialization, which yields economies of scope and scale. We see examples of this in all three organizations in this chapter. On the scope side, Asian Paints creates entire designs for its end customers, so that they can achieve a particular look or style. SSIPEX also

TABLE 9.1 Summary Comparison of Emerging Market Companies

Organization	Co-Creates with Customers	Specialization for Economies of Scope	Specialization for Economies of Scale	Openness	Changed Business Model	Comments
Asian Paints	With distributors	Yes, via new IT system	Yes	With distributors	Yes	Now has direct information from end consumer
SSIPEX	Only a broker	Yes, IP aggregator	Yes	A broker	Yes	Government owned
ShaanGu	Will design plant for customer	Yes, turnkey packages	Yes	Yes	Yes	Much closer to customer now

aggregates IP from around the world, bringing it together in one place for its clients. And ShaanGu offers turnkey packages (design, installation, operation, after-sale maintenance and support) to its clients, should they desire them. On the scale side, each organization has created standardized processes to handle transactions more efficiently.

Openness is a third theme, and we see elements of it here as well. Asian Paints is much more transparent to its distributors and applicators, allowing them to see the status of projects as it appears to them. By serving as the back office for its distribution partners, it learns a great deal more about end customers as a result. SSIPEX has made investments that let clients "try before they buy," so that they can see the outputs of the technologies they are interested in prior to making a purchase. ShaanGu is not yet at this juncture but is collecting end customer information and information about its own equipment in the field that will enable more openness down the road.

The final theme in this book refers to the need to change one's business model to take full advantage of services innovation. This is seen in all three examples. By focusing on services, each organization is moving away from a product focus, and each is striving for a more sustainable economic model. This is most obvious with Asian Paints and ShaanGu. Each is striving to move beyond commodity businesses to increase their value added to customers. SSIPEX also is part of an initiative in China to stimulate the greater use of semiconductor IP to shorten time to market for Chinese semiconductor makers. If it succeeds, it will also create ways for Chinese creators of semiconductor IP to find markets for that IP. However, none of these examples has yet reached the stage of becoming platforms to attract the participation and investment of numerous third parties. That remains an area for future work in order to sustain the growth of these entities.

Differences from Advanced Economies

Although the major themes of this book have echoes in the context of emerging economies, there also are differences. One difference we see for services innovators in less developed economies is that focusing on the end customer is often insufficient. The lack of infrastructure may limit a business's ability to service its customers, which we saw in Asian Paints in accessing remote villages, SSIPEX in the legal system supporting IP protection, and ShaanGu in its customers' ability to finance purchases of capital equipment. The distribution channels themselves also may require significant innovation investments in order to implement new services innovations. Distribution in many developing economies is inefficient, at least by the standards of developed economies. Many channel participants lack capital and know-how, are not computerized, and confront issues of stock-outs, missed appointments, or out-of-date offerings for their customers. Indeed, in order for companies to achieve the economies of scope and scale in their distribution channels in these markets, they may need to upgrade their distributors' capabilities. If the upgrading is not carefully managed to achieve a mutually desirable outcome, however, these partners may resist such attempts at it.

Instead of treating these problems as constraints, the service innovators highlighted in this chapter approached them as opportunities. Each of the examples shows the value of addressing these deficiencies as a strategy to overcome resistance to services innovations for the end customers. It may well be that this is a necessary precursor to the kinds of co-creation with end customers that we are seeing in the advanced economies. Most transactions are still taking place on a face-to-face basis in the emerging economies, and the infrastructure to reach them directly may not yet exist. Therefore, the ability to deliver services that customers expect from resellers and other third parties remains vital.

A related difference is the relative lack of well-developed capital markets. Both Asian Paints and ShaanGu have needed to offer financing to their distribution partners (and, in ShaanGu's case, its final customers) in order to support their businesses. Although this is hardly unique to the emerging economies, it may be more fundamental because alternative sources of financing for customers and distributors may be harder to come by. SSIPEX, as a government-owned organization, can work with sources of financial investment to help its clients obtain the requisite international IP for their businesses. But its use of government capital itself is being carefully metered, keeping the activity lean and focused.

A third difference is that saving labor is not a primary driver of services innovation in emerging economies. Asian Paints is not much concerned with saving time for applicators to apply its paint in India. ShaanGu has outsourced much of the most labor-intensive parts of its servicing of its equipment to other companies. It is driving itself to be more innovative in order to create and capture more value with its customers, not to save money on labor. SSIPEX worries that the legal infrastructure isn't in place to prevent piracy or obtain satisfactory enforcement should piracy activities be detected. So SSIPEX has to educate its clientele about the business benefits of pirating less and innovating faster to get to market more quickly. Speed matters more to SSIPEX than saving labor.

SUMMING UP

In this chapter, we have seen that services innovation is not unique to the developed world, an important point. I have discussed the commodity trap in advanced economies due to the rise of manufacturing output in the less developed economies. But there is also a squeeze on commodities in those less developed economies as well. In fact, both advanced and developing economies face pressures driving them to services innovations. To put the matter differently, advanced economies cannot blithely assume that they can hide behind a wall of services to avoid competing with lower-cost services-based companies from emerging markets like India or China.

If any further impetus was required to motivate companies to move toward services innovation, here it is: the world is moving toward services in both advanced and emerging economies, with or without you. Standing still in the face of these changes is not a promising option.

○ ○ ○

In the next, and final, chapter, we take a step back to examine some of the history of services innovation and explore ways in which services innovation may evolve in the near future. We also consider some of the issues and challenges for companies in pursuing Open Services Innovation.

CHAPTER 10

OPEN SERVICES INNOVATION: THE WAY FORWARD

Most of this book has looked at services innovation for individual firms. This chapter explores the larger context in which the shift toward services innovation is taking place. It looks back in history to put services innovation into a larger context, examines some of the issues and concerns that arise around services innovation, and considers industry trends that are driving services innovation forward. This chapter, and the book, conclude with a discussion of Open Services Innovation, and why it is the best way forward for both leading firms that want to grow and compete as well as for advanced economies.

As of this writing, the global economic system is showing some signs of a possible start of turnaround especially in business services, but it is still a mess. Advanced economies are saddled with too much debt relative to the size of their economies. Social safety nets are at risk as countries cut spending significantly in order to reverse the increasing burden of debt. Newly emerging economies like China, India, and Brazil are growing much faster than the advanced economies of member countries of the Organization for Economic Cooperation and Development. A new economic order is being fashioned as the G-8 (China and other emerging economies are not represented) is giving way to the G-20 (where these emerging countries are represented). Yet these emerging countries have their own significant unmet social needs and worry about instability and conflict within their own borders as well as overdependence on more developed nations.

The only way out of this mess in the long term is growth. Only when economies grow can there be sufficient resources to meet the needs of today's citizens while providing the resources to nurture and educate tomorrow's citizens. Continuous innovation is the only sustainable growth policy to get us there. Our economic future clearly depends on creating and advancing innovation.

That brings us to services. Services are the next frontier in innovation. Much of the future growth that is going to support economic prosperity will come from services innovations. This will be true not only in today's advanced economies but also the emerging economies that will be advanced economies in their own right in the near future. As our economies continue to become more globally connected, we are increasingly dependent on each other to generate innovation and prosperity throughout the world.

INNOVATION IN HISTORIC CONTEXT

It's important to put services innovation into a larger historic context: looking back helps to see more clearly into the future. Until a century ago, services simply weren't very important to economic activity. Most people around the world worked on farms, and most of the food grown on these farms was consumed by the farmers who grew the food and by their neighbors. When times were good, there was plenty of food. When times were hard, millions of people went without. Prolonged difficult conditions could lead to hard times, even mass starvation. (In the Irish potato famine, more than 1 million people died and another 1 million fled, reducing Ireland's population by more than 20 percent in just seven years.)

Today there is plenty of food and little subsistence agriculture left in the advanced economies of the world. Instead, the vastly greater output of farms today is grown for sale and export, to be consumed at a later time, quite far from the farm that grew the food. The difference between those outcomes lies in innovations that created the incredible productivity increases we have enjoyed in agriculture and, more recently, in manufacturing. Although there remain important issues of distribution of food, land use, and sustainable practices, we are living longer and healthier lives at a higher standard of living because of these increases in comparison to a century ago.[1]

This happened for a number of reasons. One is that agricultural productivity increased with the rise of knowledge-intensive, specialized industries that support this productivity: farm equipment manufacturing, fertilizers and pesticide manufacturing, seeds with superior genetic characteristics, land management practices, better price signaling markets for commodities, transportation systems, fuel supply systems, and more. The government helped too. Agricultural research stations were created to apply new knowledge to local farming conditions. Often these were housed in land grant colleges, which were funded by national and state governments to promote greater education in farming (and, later, in engineering as well). Farm bureaus, futures markets, price supports, and other policies promoted, expanded, and stabilized markets for agricultural products. Farming thus shifted from subsistence farming (growing what one needed in order to eat) to specialized farming focused on one or two cash crops (and buying what one needed to eat).

In sum, vast new bodies of knowledge embedded in new institutions developed to support a much smaller population of farmers. These new bodies of knowledge provided services to farmers, and these services have greatly increased the productivity of farms. As a result, we have gone from subsistence farming, to industrial farming, to abundance.

Something similar has happened to manufacturing, again thanks to innovation. The rise of information technologies has supported the development of factory automation as well as global export markets. Global communication networks allow products to be built in factories and workshops all over the world. Companies can simultaneously be closer to their customers' needs in local markets, while providing up-to-the-minute information to their production networks for what products are needed, where they are needed, and in what quantity. The fields of engineering (civil, mechanical, electrical, industrial, nuclear, systems, and, most recently, bioengineering) arose in colleges and universities around the world to support the design, development, and production of a myriad assortment of products. These are also services, which again contributed to the productivity of the manufacturing sector.

The important lesson in this is that innovation plays a critical role in economic prosperity, and the full benefit of innovation often is apparent only after the fact. Innovation, moreover, shows scant regard for traditional boundaries, such as agriculture, manufacturing, and services. Today's advanced economies live in a postmanufacturing world. A vast array of services today comprises nearly 80 percent of U.S. economic activity and a similar magnitude of economic activity in other advanced economies in Asia and Europe.[2] Services today are responsible for the majority of employment in the OECD countries, and their portion of these economies is increasing. Our future prosperity will come from learning how to manage this shift from a product-based economy to a largely services-based economy, driven by innovating in the services sector of the economy and transforming the product sector of the economy in the process.

We also must look at some of the issues that services innovation must confront to assess its potential to increase its own productivity (versus its contributions to other sectors like agriculture and manufacturing). Since it is more than 80 percent of economic activity, it must learn to innovate itself, in addition to other sectors, if economic growth is to continue.

ISSUES IN SERVICES INNOVATION

Because of the intangible nature of services, observing them directly and measuring accordingly is difficult. There has even been an academic debate about whether services could in fact be innovated due to these concerns. Throughout this book, I have followed the definition I gave in Chapter Two about "a change in the condition of a person, or a good belonging to some economic entity." Although this definition isn't perfect, it has the virtue of being the one under which most economic data have been collected. These data do measure services and do suggest that services (in some areas) are improving productivity.

191

Another concern has been the uneven advance of productivity in services. Although some sectors, such as the retail sector, have increased their productivity, other service sectors have not. One concern is Baumol's disease, a term coined by economist William Baumol to describe an economy in which the efficient sectors that contribute to productivity over an extended period of time become a smaller part of the overall economy, while less efficient sectors come to dominate economic activity.[3] In many services, for example, it is hard to envision the kinds of dramatic productivity gains observed in agriculture and manufacturing. Consider the fields of education, health care, and government, which are hard to standardize and are dominated by labor costs. If those fields remain laggards, they will grow in relation to the more efficient sectors of the economy. But their growing share of the economy is a sign of a weakness (an inability to streamline and improve their activities relative to other sectors of the economy), not a strength.

For a specific example of Baumol's disease in action, consider health care in the United States. Health care amounts to more than 17 percent of the U.S. gross domestic product, double its percentage from a generation ago. Although treatments for acute diseases have advanced tremendously in the past generation, chronic diseases are rising rapidly. As a result, overall public health measures for U.S. citizens like infant mortality, life spans, and morbidity rates have not advanced much, if at all. This lack of improvement comes despite an enormous increase in health care funding in the United States during that period in absolute dollars and as a proportion of the total economy. The United States leads the world in health care spending, both in the aggregate and per person, yet its health outcomes are below those of most of the other advanced world economies. The productivity gap in this area of services requires innovation for it to improve.

A Need for Services Innovation Research

To close the productivity gap in services in areas like health care, we need to stimulate much greater research activity in the university sector toward services innovation. The productivity gains of the past have arisen from the research and development efforts of the private, public, and academic sectors. At the heart of this R&D system is the university and the group of scholars, students, and alumni who comprise the greater academic community, with students moving on to all sectors. As I discussed in *Open Innovation,* there has been a shift in the innovation system in which large corporate labs are increasingly focused on projects with a shorter time horizon.[4] Universities are increasingly the locus of basic research in most advanced economies, so we must look there for the research that will drive innovation in services in the long term.

In services, however, no academic community of scholars shares a common mission to understand the roots of the services arena of economic activity or how to advance it. Granted, services subfields are emerging in separate, siloed academic areas, but precious few attempts to integrate them have been undertaken, and this is much needed.[5]

Since we now live in a services-based economy, it is disconcerting that universities are not focused on the vital services sector in their research activity. At a time when concerns about outsourcing and offshoring white-collar jobs and economic development are raising alarms, a field that could assist in understanding how to add value and jobs goes unexplored. Our ability to achieve a further rise in our standard of living requires a deeper understanding of how to innovate in services.

One explanation for why academics have been slow to change their perspective on the importance of services in the economy is proposed by Stephen Vargo and Robert Lusch.[6] They argue that the result of two centuries of focusing on economic goods is a traditional goods-centered dominant logic in economics and business thinking.[7] Even the accounting system used to track and record business performance is trapped in a product context. There is careful tracking of inventory, for example, from raw material, to work in process, to final goods. But accounting systems provide no reporting of renewal rates, employee turnover, customer satisfaction, on-time delivery, or similar key measures associated with services performance.

Other reasons are holding back universities, in the United States and elsewhere, from developing strong research in the services area.

Although some good work has been published on services innovation, universities are constructed not to change quickly. Part of the university's longevity, a great strength, derives from its resistance to sudden change. This can become a weakness when economic activity is shifting to a new area—and we live in a new era of turbulent rapid change. The partitions of knowledge that exist in most universities have grown up, and perhaps congealed, around the agricultural and manufacturing worlds. There are extensive agricultural research domains (agronomy, biology, ecology) and manufacturing research domains (such as the many kinds of engineering now taught in universities around the world). These are well established and defended by tenured faculty who are experts in those knowledge domains and skeptical of any new trends that threaten their hegemony.[8]

Roland Rust, one of the pioneers of services marketing and himself a marketing professor, recently made a call for integration in an editorial in *The Journal of Services Research*, which he founded and edits: "The field of service research is inherently interdisciplinary, and we can move the field forward not only by understanding and serving the customer (service marketing...) but by designing efficient systems of service delivery (service operations...); training and motivating service providers (service HR...); using new service technologies (service MIS...); and understanding how service affects the marketplace, the economy, and government policy (service economics)."[9]

Over the past two decades, a number of European countries have done a great deal of work to understand the growth of their services sector and try to increase government investment in services. However, the approaches to service innovation, despite many solid contributions, have remained balkanized in different academic disciplines.[10] No unified model that unites and inspires these different disciplines has yet emerged. It seems unlikely that systematic approaches to services innovation can be achieved without an interdisciplinary effort that unites academic silos around a common set of problems.

Services are different from these earlier partitions of knowledge and can add value in both agriculture and manufacturing contexts. But they have the potential to be more than tools to support the earlier knowledge partitions. Services innovation can become a new way to think about innovation in an increasingly knowledge-based economy. And these new ways of thinking do not comport well with the earlier knowledge partitions that delineate university departments.

The current approach of government funding for services innovation research isn't helping to improve the situation. According to a study by the National Academy of Engineering, federal funding agencies do not fund long-range, high-impact academic research in services fields such as logistics because these agencies do not see services as a separate intellectual discipline. The same study asserts that "the U.S. academic research enterprise is not focused and organized to meet the needs of service businesses."[11] Even the Defense Advanced Research Projects Agency, which traditionally has been one of the most far-sighted, long-range funders of basic research, has chosen to give most of its funding in research for the logistics services industry to consulting companies rather than to universities. When one of the leading funders of long-term research does this, it is a telling indictment of the perceived lack of relevance of the U.S. academic research enterprise in the services domain.[12] The lack of a coherent, integrated approach to services innovation is a missed opportunity—one that could limit the future growth of advanced economies, which are increasingly based on services.

If we can create a shared agenda of research focused on the services sector, this need not continue. Through developing common terminology and agreement on multiple methods that increase our insight into the services domain, we can reconnect universities to the dominant economic activities of the larger society that supports them. We may also uncover ways to increase high-value, high-wage employment that supports an abundant and rising standard of living.

Transcending the Boundaries of Services Silos

The leading role of services in the economy comes as no surprise to many companies that previously were admired leaders in the manufacturing sector. Manufacturers such as GE, Xerox, and IBM find that services constitute the fastest-growing parts of their business today. Indeed, IBM receives the majority of its revenues from its IBM Global Services Business, a unit that did not exist prior to the 1990s. But the companies that have been leading the charge themselves often lack a strong conceptual foundation for their work. Although they call their work *services* (following the agriculture/manufacturing/services taxonomy), most practitioners of services consulting divide their areas into domains or vertical markets, such as financial services, health care, transportation, government, education, and so forth. They follow these groupings because they correspond to the customer markets that they serve with their offerings. But this is due to marketing considerations, not to any shared concept of the underlying structure of the offerings they provide. The lack of any more general understanding of the essence of their offerings inhibits their ability to make advances.

There is an interesting analogy to be made between the evolution of services innovation and the evolution of computer architectures. In the early days of the computer industry, mainframe computers from different manufacturers were targeted to specific applications, and there were no facilities to share data, programming, or other elements among them. These different systems correspond to today's vertical silos in services, where little is shared among the different service domains (see Figure 10.1).

FIGURE 10.1   Vertical Silos in the Services Sector

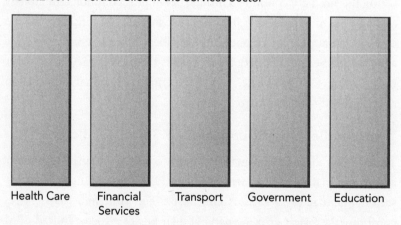

Health Care   Financial   Transport   Government   Education
               Services

FIGURE 10.2   A Vision of Services Tomorrow

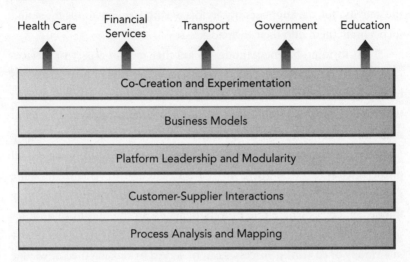

Today's computing architectures are moving toward the cloud, an environment in which devices of various sizes, shapes, manufacturers, and operating systems can access, share, store, and manage data and applications. There is lots of sharing across all of these architectures, and that is where services innovation will be heading in the future. The ideas in this book will enable services to learn, share, and improve across the boundaries of those silos, so that co-creation in one domain will inform co-creation in another domain, and so forth (see Figure 10.2).

Academic research might be helpful in the process of breaking down these silos, as it has been in both agriculture and manufacturing (and the computer industry). One area where academics might help is in managing complex knowledge. Services innovation in each of the vertical markets involves many complex combinations of knowledge. Indeed the very prevalence of so many pieces of information results in a challenging problem: how to create systems that combine these pieces into coherent solutions. And because it is a challenging problem, the ability to solve it is becoming an increasingly important source of economic value. The questions of how to partition the complex knowledge, how to integrate it, and how to coordinate the recombination and reuse of knowledge from one instance into a new instance are fundamental to the economics of the activity, for the suppliers of services and those who adopt them and incorporate them into their own businesses.

Transforming business models is another critical aspect of services innovation. Academic research can assist in refining the concept of business process modeling. This technique deconstructs a business model that commercializes a technology into constituent business processes and maps interactions among these processes.[13] Like the question of managing complex combinations of knowledge, this technique is useful across all of the vertical markets. These maps are an attempt to visualize how the different activities in a business process connect to one another, including the dependencies where one process depends on the output of another process or feeds into yet another. Ideally, elements that recur frequently in a variety of customer processes can be served by reusing the knowledge employed to accomplish that element in a different process. This enables commonly shared elements to be recombined in a variety of ways to serve a variety of potential purposes.

Integration in Services

Complex offerings are where integration skills become so important in services. Product-based businesses leave it to the customer to perform the final installation and integration of the item into his or her process. Service businesses deliver the benefit to the customer by taking over the integration of the item. A company like Best Buy makes some margin from selling a big screen TV. But Best Buy makes much more margin from delivering that TV, hooking it up to the cable or satellite service, programming the TV and its remote control, possibly connecting it with the home stereo system, taking away the old TV, and selling a warranty that lets customers call Best Buy if and when anything goes wrong.

And this is a good deal for customers too. They might buy a new TV once every five or ten years. They have to figure out this integration again every time because the technology has changed since the last time they bought a TV. But Best Buy is delivering, installing, and supporting thousands of TVs every day. Over time, its people develop significant competence and skill in performing these tasks that most customers could not hope to acquire, even if they had the time and inclination. So Best Buy can provide a valuable service to customers at an affordable price and dramatically increase its profits from the engagement.

Effective integration can even create value for the customer and reduce costs for the supplier at the same time. One example is the systems integrator Alstom, which designs, manufactures, and operates the subway cars for one line of the London Underground (also known as the Tube). From its experience operating the vehicles it designed, in consultation with the London Tube Authority, the company identified 250 product improvements that increased the uptime of its cars. These improvements also reduced their service costs over their expected thirty years of use. This enabled the Tube Authority to reduce the number of extra cars kept on hand as spares (thus saving money for the supplier Alstom), while improving uptime availability of the service, and thus service quality for the Tube.[14]

A supplier can take on the challenges of systems integration and make money while still giving a better deal to the customer only if the customer is able to alter its own operations as a result of having the supplier provide a complete solution. For example, the customer may no longer require an in-house maintenance crew or an internal IT staff (as in the case of IBM), an internal shipping department (in the case of UPS), or spare parts and maintenance departments (as in the case of Alstom and the London Tube Authority). The ability to streamline operations can lead to win-win outcomes in services innovation. This is a further dimension in co-creation between customer and supplier: the dimension of improving or eliminating customer processes and taking costs out of the system.

Ultimately understanding how to innovate in services will enhance the productivity of companies, and of society. We know from the work of Eric Brynjolfsson and Robert Gordon, among others, in studying macroeconomic statistics, that a key driver in the variation in productivity of different industries lies in the ways in which companies have incorporated new communications and information technologies into their businesses.[15] As Brynjolfsson and Yang wrote, "Wal-Mart's main assets are not their computer software and hardware, but the intangible business processes they have built around those computer systems."[16]

This is the sweet spot for the study of services innovation for both academics and companies. Any useful answers to why services companies vary in their intangible business processes will invariably involve concepts that cut across vertical services markets (see Figure 10.2). A deep understanding of customer needs, including customer insights, empathic understanding of unmet needs, the customer's own business model, and key processes, also will be required. Understanding how to innovate in the largest and fastest-growing area of most advanced economies could be the call to action that unites the many stakeholders who must break out of disciplinary or functional silos. We need to unite around common problems to make more rapid progress.

This is a daunting research agenda, but there is no alternative in a services-led economy. As IBM Research's former senior vice president, Paul Horn, notes, "We need to overcome the silos of departments and disciplines if we are going to generate the innovation needed in a services economy."

THE WAY FORWARD

Let's return to where I began this book. Globalization continues to advance, creating more competition but also expanding markets around the world. This creates obvious threats to established companies, challenges for smaller ones, and pressures on wages of lesser-skilled workers in advanced economies. The commoditization trap is going to continue to operate and may even intensify in the coming years. Growth will continue to be hard. Product-focused companies are going to struggle if they confine their innovations to products alone. Services-focused companies will also struggle if they cannot scale their services to grow profitably through innovation so that revenues grow faster than the costs.

Yet the emergence of a billion or more new consumers into the global market is a genuinely exciting prospect. As these people earn higher wages, their ability and desire to consume will increase. Their time will become more valuable to them. And they will not only want to buy more products, they will demand the services that wrap around these products. They too will want experiences, not just stuff.

The increased market provided by these new consumers will stimulate greater specialization in both economies of scale and of scope and enable companies to thrive on being part of a global innovation services chain without having to provide all the links in the chain themselves. The supply of services innovations will be expanded, and the expanded market will be there to reward those who provide them. No doubt innovative companies based in emerging economies will be looked to to serve the needs of new customers, while some governments will look to set indigenous innovation policy preferences to encourage them. But innovation cannot be kept in a bottle, and there will be plenty of opportunities to construct new platforms with both local and nonlocal participants.

Innovation itself is also going global. Many multinational companies have already established extensive R&D facilities in a number of countries. They have done this not only to access the local market, but also to tap into the increasingly skilled and capable local talent in those markets. We are now seeing reverse innovation, where new products are being created in developing economies and exported to the advanced economies.[17] And we see hybrid organizations that are doing all of the above in hopes of getting the best of both worlds.

This is no time to be timid. This increasingly demanding global environment will provide rich rewards to those who take bold steps to harness the global market for ideas, technology, talent, and, yes, services. By inviting customers to co-create with you, you can foster differentiated, meaningful experiences for your customers that increase your own profits. By embracing the Open Services Innovation approach, you can get the best external ideas joined to your best internal ideas and take those combinations to new markets. You can invest in deepening economies of scale to lower your costs while pursuing economies of scope to build stronger, more profitable relationships with your customers. By transforming your business model into a platform to make the most of services innovation, you can sustain your profitability and make it harder for your competitors to displace you.

This is the way forward. Open Services Innovation will lift you out of the commodity trap enabling you to grow and compete on entirely new levels where your customers and other businesses rely on you, benefit from working with you, and help you move into a brighter future.

It is high time to get started on the journey.

INTRODUCTION

1. For an extensive view of data on services, see Organization for Economic Cooperation and Development, "The Service Economy" (Paris: Organization for Economic Cooperation and Development, 2000), http://www .oecd.org/dataoecd/10/33/2090561.pdf.

2. Uday Apte, Uday Karmarkar, and Hiranya Nath carefully decompose U.S. economic statistics into a "double dichotomy of Information Products and Services, and Material Products and Services." Their analysis demonstrates that the bulk of economic growth in the U.S. economy over the past fifty years comes from the two quadrants of information—information-intensive products and information-intensive services—with the latter providing the largest growth in jobs and value added to the economy. See their "Information Services in the US Economy," *California Management Review*, Spring 2008, pp. 12–30.

3. These tools include component business modeling (which we will see in Chapter Five), solution design management, and intelligent document gateway, respectively. I am indebted to my colleague Jim Spohrer at IBM for these examples of IBM's service innovation achievements.

Notes

CHAPTER 1

1. See the *Forbes* magazine "Four Hundred Richest People" issue, Mar. 3, 2010, http://www.forbes.com/2010/03/10/worlds-richest-people-slim-gates-buffett-billionaires-2010_land.html. Hong Kong is counted as part of China in these data; Taiwan is not.

2. This was highlighted in P. Orszag, "Birth Date, Business Cycles, and Lifetime Income" (Washington, D.C.: Office of Management and Budget, Oct. 2009), http://www.whitehouse.gov/omb/blog/09/10/22/Birth-date-business-cycles-and-lifetime-income/.

3. See Richard D'Aveni's book *Beating the Commodity Trap* (Boston: Harvard Business School Press, 2010) for a discussion of the commodity trap. The key idea behind the trap is that the innovative process that companies followed in the past will no longer take them into a prosperous future. As the saying goes, "What got you here won't get you there." D'Aveni identifies four types of the trap: from deterioration to proliferation to escalation, and finally evaporation. The discussion in this book is closest to the deterioration trap.

4. National Academy of Engineering, *The Impact of Academic Research on Industrial Performance* (Washington, D.C.: National Academies Press, 2003).

5. Organization for Economic Cooperation and Development, "The Service Economy" (Paris: Organization for Economic Cooperation and Development, 2000), http://www.oecd.org/dataoecd/10/33/2090561.pdf.

6. The facts in this paragraph about the Motorola Razr are from Wikipedia: http://en.wikipedia.org/wiki/Razr.

7. An analyst estimates that Motorola's market share in cell phones has fallen from 16 percent in 2005, during the success of the Razr, to under 5 percent. "Motorola's Stock Extremely Sensitive to Changes in Mobile Phone Share," *Seeking Alpha*, July 26, 2010, http://seekingalpha.com/article/216528-motorolas-stock-extremely-sensitive-to-changes-in-mobile-phone-market-share.

8. The challenge facing Nokia's organization can been seen in its opening of a research lab next to the Berkeley campus in November 2009. When I interviewed the lab managers, they were proud of the rigorous metrics used to evaluate the performance of the lab. These metrics were based

foremost on patent applications and also academic papers and conference presentations. These metrics fit well with the product world, but they fit poorly with the need to develop and stimulate new applications and services, where patents will be of little importance. In my view, this brand-new lab was hamstrung from the start by its management metrics.

9. Apple's iPhone became a vital platform, but Steve Jobs didn't view it that way initially. As Wade Roush describes it in xconomy.com on Jan. 25, 2010, Apple's thinking about the iPhone evolved quite a bit after its market introduction: "Shortly after the iPhone was announced in January 2007, Steve Jobs told the *New York Times*: 'We define everything that is on the phone. You don't want your phone to be like a PC. The last thing you want is to have loaded three apps on your phone and then you go to make a call and it doesn't work anymore. These are more like iPods than they are like computers.' By 2008, though, Jobs had apparently realized that in its quest to 'define everything,' the company was leaving a lot of money on the table. The 120,000 apps you can now find in the iTunes App Store—with Apple collecting 30 percent of every paid-app sale—are testimony to the wisdom of the shift." This shows the value of co-creation, one of the key themes in this book: the chance for others to complete the work that you started, going well beyond what you envisioned or intended. Even perfectionist Steve Jobs realized the value of letting others into the Apple innovation process.

10. From an interview with Kevin Fong of Mayfield Fund, on Sand Hill Road in Menlo Park. The interview was held in his office on Feb. 3, 2005.

11. See Inder Sidhu's book *Doing Both: How Cisco Captures Today's Profit and Drives Tomorrow's Growth* (Upper Saddle River, N.J.: FT Press, 2010) as one documented case where Cisco manages both parts of this trade-off with some success.

12. As Andrew Davies, Michael Hobday, and Andrea Prencipe have shown in "Systems Integration: A Core Capability of the Modern Corporation," *Industrial and Corporate Change*, 2006, *14*, 1109–1143, the proportion of standardized and customized elements in a solution will vary according to the nature of the market (for example, lower-volume industrial products or high-volume consumer goods). In high-volume industries, the product is usually offered as only a standardized bundle, including a predefined

set of services. In complex industrial settings, the solution offered varies considerably depending on the needs, capabilities, and sophistication of the customer organizations. Less experienced customers with limited internal systems-related capabilities often demand solutions consisting entirely of standardized offerings. More experienced or sophisticated customers, by contrast, may find that their needs are not met by a standardized solution.

13. Professor Ikujiro Nonaka has led the way in connecting the importance of tacit knowledge to innovation. See his excellent book with Hiro-taki Takeuchi, *The Knowledge Creating Company* (New York: Oxford University Press, 1995). In their formulation, codified knowledge represents information that is well understood by providers and customers, such as specifications and standards. Companies can develop their offerings according to these specs and be confident that their customers will be able to use their offerings so long as the customers follow the same specs. Examples of such technical standards include the html and http protocols for the Internet and the digital video disk format for movies. Such widely shared information cannot be the basis for competitive advantage. Instead, it is the ability to elicit tacit knowledge that provides a competitive edge for firms.

14. See Susumu Ogawa and Frank Pillar's excellent article on Threadless: "Reducing the Risks of New Product Development," *Sloan Management Review*, Winter 2006, pp. 65–71.

15. S. Cook, "The Contribution Revolution," *Harvard Business Review*, Oct. 2008, pp. 60–69. Scott Cook is one of the most thoughtful entrepreneurs. He not only founded and grew Intuit to its current success but fought off Bill Gates and Microsoft in doing so. He now sits on the board of Procter & Gamble. He is well worth reading on user contributions and other topics.

16. See the prescient book by Joseph Pine and James Gilmore, *The Experience Economy* (Boston: Harvard Business School Press, 1999), for an early articulation of the role that subjective experiences play in advanced economies. They also develop the concept of experience points: points of contact between customers and suppliers in the exchange of services, where each entity's respective processes interact in order to accomplish

the exchange. At each of these experience points, customers select paths from sets of choices constructed by suppliers, and the exchanges branch into different areas depending on the customer's choice. They can be thought of as moments of truth, where customers see what the service is really like for them at that moment.

17. See my book, *Open Innovation: The New Imperative for Creating and Profiting from Technology* (Boston: Harvard Business School Press, 2003), for a discussion on the value of open innovation approaches in research and development. My later book, *Open Business Models: How to Thrive in the New Innovation Landscape* (Boston: Harvard Business School Press, 2006), extends open innovation to business model innovation and intellectual property as well. Daniel Fasnacht wrote his doctoral dissertation on how open innovation influences financial services; it has been published with the catchy title *Open Innovation in Financial Services* (New York: Springer, 2009). From a user perspective, Eric von Hippel's work is also instructive about the value users add to the innovation process. His classic work is *The Sources of Innovation* (New York: Oxford University Press, 1988), which is significantly updated and extended in *Democratizing Innovation* (Cambridge, Mass.: MIT Press, 2005).

18. I am indebted to my colleague Andrew Davies at Imperial College, London, for the example of the BBC documented here. See his article with John Bessant, "Managing Service Innovation," in J. Bessant and others (eds.), *Innovation in Services* (London: Department of Trade and Industry, 2007).

19. Carliss Baldwin and Kim Clark's book *Design Rules* (Cambridge, Mass.: MIT Press, 2000) develops an elegant argument along these lines. This book is well worth the time required to grasp the authors' presentation of the idea of modularity in systems.

20. Velcade's innovative pricing is documented in A. Pollack, "Pricing Pills by the Results," *New York Times,* July 14, 2007, http://www.nytimes.com/2007/07/14/business/14drugprice.html?pagewanted=print.

CHAPTER 2

1. "Service" in *Oxford Dictionaries,* http://www.askoxford.com/concise_oed/service?view=uk.

2. E. Pearce, *History of the Standard Industrial Classification* (Washington, D.C.: Executive Office of the President/Office of Statistical Standards, U.S. Bureau of the Budget, 1957).

3. T. P. Hill, "On Goods and Services," *Review of Income and Wealth,* 1977, *23*, 315–338.

4. See M. Mohr's "NAPCS Structure Illustration: Possible Product Groups, Sub-Groups, and Classes," NAPCS discussion paper (Apr. 2003), http://www.census.gov/eos/www/napcs/papers/structured.pdf. Other definitions of *services* in this same spirit can be found in P. Kotler and P. Bloom, *Marketing Professional Services* (Upper Saddle River, N.J.: Prentice Hall, 1984). Both emphasize an exchange between two or more parties, resulting in a transformation received by the customer and also note the intangible nature of the exchange between the supplier and the customer.

5. For an argument that services innovation is not very different from product innovation, see P. Vermeulen and W. Van de Aa, "Organizing Services Innovation," in I. Miles and J. Tidd (eds.), *Service Innovation: Organizational Responses to Technological Imperatives and Market Opportunities* (London: Imperial College Press, 2003).

6. M. Porter, *Competitive Advantage* (New York: Free Press, 1985).

7. T. Levitt, "Marketing Myopia," *Harvard Business Review*, July–Aug. 1960, pp. 45–56. Peter Drucker's quote comes from his wonderful book *Management: Tasks, Responsibilities, Practices* (Burlington, Mass.: Butterworth-Heinemann, 1999), p. 57, first published in 1974 .

8. I am grateful to my friend and colleague Rich Mironov for suggesting the metaphor for this section. He did so in his series of blog postings, Product Bytes, which can be found at www.mironov.com and are compiled into his self-published book, *The Art of Product Management: Lessons from a Silicon Valley Entrepreneur* (2008).

9. See B. Kümin, "Eating Out Before the Restaurant: Dining Cultures in Early-Modern Inns," in M. Jacobs and Peter Scholliers (eds.), *Eating Out in Europe: Picnics, Gourmet Dining and Snacks Since the Late Eighteenth Century* (New York: Berg, 2003). Note that the rise of restaurants exemplifies a key theme in this book: that consumers of sufficient income desire variety and seek out solutions that reduce their hidden costs. Although the market for foodstuffs may be somewhat limited by the

caloric intake needs of the world's population, the market for restaurants to create new combinations of food is vastly larger. By contrast, when economic growth slows or goes into recession, discretionary consumption at restaurants goes down as well.

10. This description of El Bulli follows a paper I jointly authored in Spanish with Francesco Sandulli of the Complutense University of Madrid: "The Two Sides of Open Business Models," *Universia Business Review*, 2009, pp. 12–39. A near-equivalent English-language working paper can be found in the Social Science Research Network: F. D. Sandulli and H. Chesbrough, "The Two Sides of Open Business Models," Jan. 10, 2009, http://ssrn.com/abstract=1325682.

11. This example is adapted from my chapter "Constructing and Managing Innovation in Business Networks" in J. Word (ed.), *Business Network Transformation* (San Francisco: Jossey-Bass, 2009).

12. See A. Saxenian, *The New Argonauts* (Berkeley: University of California Press, 2005), for an extended discussion of Taiwan's rapid development generally and the powerful role that TSMC played in particular to help create this growth. This book contains many other valuable insights and is well worth reading.

13. M. LaPedus, Apr. 30, 2008, http://www.eetasia.com/login.do? fromWhere=/ART_8800520035_480100_NT_2f1c5bcb.HTM.

CHAPTER 3

1. I am not claiming that all customers do this. I only claim that some portion of customers do perform such comparisons. In addition, resources like Consumer Reports, JD Power and Associates, Gartner Associates (in the information technology world), and other similar organizations can act as an independent assessor of products for customers.

2. Professor Ikujiro Nonaka's excellent book with Hirotaki Takeuchi, *The Knowledge Creating Company* (New York: Oxford University Press, 1995).

3. The classic example of tacit knowledge, taken from M. Polanyi, *The Tacit Dimension* (New York: Doubleday, 1966), is learning to ride a bicycle.

4. C. Hays, "What Walmart Knows About Customers' Habits," From *The New York Times*, © Nov. 14, 2004. All rights reserved. Used by permission and protected by the Copyright Laws of the United States.

5. Eric von Hippel at MIT has done some fascinating work on user tool kits. The example of Lego given here is quite consistent with this work. The basic concept is powerful and simple. Users are creative and innovative, and organizations simply need to give them the tools to create exciting possibilities, then let them modify and recombine as they wish. This is a powerful way to tap into innovation possibilities that traditional market research might never uncover. A moment's reflection, however, helps us realize that users cannot be simply turned loose; instead, they need to be directed to focus on particular areas within certain boundaries. This is where the tool kits come in. The tool kits package possible service offerings into different items that users can mix and match as they wish. But confining the users to the items available places some limits on what users do with these possibilities. Tool kits thus put certain boundary conditions on these variations, so that they remain feasible to produce and safe to consume. See E. von Hippel, "User Toolkits for Innovation," *Journal of Product Innovation Management,* 2001, *18,* 247–257.

6. See M. J. Bitner, A. Ostrom, and F. Morgan, "Service Blueprinting," *California Management Review,* 2008, *50*(3), 66–94.

7. See http://www.gigwise.com/news/38378/majority-download-radioheads-in-rainbows-for-free.

8. R. Brunner, "You Say You Want a Revolution," *Entertainment Weekly,* Oct. 23, 2007. The article further explains the traditional record company view of the Radiohead experiment: "L.A. Reid is not happy. The chairman of the Island Def Jam Music Group—the man behind Usher, Kanye West, and Mariah Carey's comeback—thinks Radiohead are making a terrible mistake. 'I'm a huge Radiohead fan, love their music,' says Reid, puffing on a cigar behind an imposing desk in his midtown New York office. 'But I think it's irresponsible on Radiohead's part to take the position that they don't need a record company. Because it may work for a few artists who are hugely successful, but the large population of recording artists aren't Radiohead.' What especially irks Reid is the band's implicit devaluation of recorded music. 'To give away music is a huge mistake,' he says. 'Because the music they make is amazing. They should charge more for their record. Because it's better! I think it's a horrible signal to

send out. I'm a huge fan of their music, but I absolutely question their business acumen.'"

9. "Free Album Divides Music Industry," SBS World News Headlines, Oct. 12, 2007. See also C. Anderson, *Free: The Future of a Radical Price* (New York: Hyperion, 2009), for a thoughtful discussion of the various ways in which "free" can be used to create more value and more sales for businesses.

10. Howard is quoted in J. Yerger, "Radiohead Experiment Continues," *Villanova University U-Wire,* Jan. 31, 2008.

11. See C. Shih, *The Facebook Era* (Upper Saddle River, N.J.: Prentice Hall, 2010), for a discussion of MySpace's evolution and its importance as a site for fans to find their favorite bands, and vice versa.

CHAPTER 4

1. H. Chesbrough, *Open Innovation* (Boston: Harvard Business School Press, 2003).

2. Open innovation is sometimes conflated with open source methodologies for software development. There are some concepts that are shared between the two, such as the idea of greater external sources of information to create value. However, open innovation explicitly incorporates the business model as the source of both value creation and value capture. This latter role of the business model enables the organization to sustain its position in the industry value chain over time. While open source shares the focus on value creation throughout an industry value chain, its proponents usually deny or downplay the importance of value capture. For more on these distinctions, see J. West and M. Bogers, "Contrasting Innovation Creation and Commercialization Within Open, User and Cumulative Innovation" (paper presented at the Academy of Management, Montreal, 2010).

3. H. Chesbrough, W. Vanhaverbeke, and J. West, *Open Innovation: Researching a New Paradigm* (New York: Oxford University Press, 2006), p. 1.

4. These data are for the United States. T. Friedman, *The World Is Flat: A Brief History of the Twenty-First Century* (New York: Farrar, Straus &

Giroux, 2005), carries this argument through to an international level. Although his data are largely anecdotal, Friedman's claim that "the world is flat" is another way of saying that there are fewer economies of scale in R&D globally as well as in the United States, creating a more level playing field for non-U.S. firms to compete.

5. See George Stigler's classic article: "The Division of Labor Is Limited by the Extent of the Market," *Journal of Political Economy*, 1951, *59*, 185–193. Here he expounds on the idea that specialization, or the division of labor, depends on the size of the market. I am arguing that the causality can also run the other way in the services context.

6. My colleague at Berkeley, Oliver Williamson, shared the Nobel Prize in 2009 for his own work on transactions costs that extended Coase's work. I was fortunate enough to have him as a teacher during my doctoral program at Berkeley.

7. As an indication of this, the original mass storage device that IBM invented for its System 360 mainframe computers in 1956 was called the RAMAC, an acronym for random access memory for accounting and control. As the name suggests, the early uses of the RAMAC were for accounting functions in businesses that could afford a computer. It took many more years for computers to become general tools that could be applied to lots of kinds of activities.

8. See H. Chesbrough and D. Teece, "When Is Virtual Virtuous?" *Harvard Business Review*, June 1996, pp. 45–54. This article provides an analysis of these issues and why outsourcing everything is not a sustainable business strategy.

9. See Paul Romer's important article that formalized this insight: "Increasing Returns and Long-Run Growth," *Journal of Political Economy*, 1986, *94*(5), 1002–1037.

10. This term harkens back to J. Panzar and R. Willig, "Economies of Scope," *American Economic Review*, 1981, *71*, 268–272. In comparison with earlier works on economies of scale, the concept of economies of scope is much more recent.

11. This is an example of two-sided markets. The more one side of the market develops (such as the number and variety of songs available on iTunes), the more attractive that becomes to customers (who are the other side

of the market). And of course, the more customers who come to the iTunes site, the more desirable the iTunes site is for new music to be distributed there. Each side of the market reinforces the other when a two-sided market develops. Equally, the lack of one side of the market can thwart the ability of the other side of the market to develop. For an introduction to this concept, see T. Eisenmann, G. Parker, and M. Van Alstyne, "Strategies for Two-Sided Markets," *Harvard Business Review*, Oct. 2006, pp. 92–101. In September 2009, Apple announced that more than 2 billion apps had been downloaded from its Apps Store to the iPhone and that more than 80,000 apps were now available for sale in its Apps Store.

12. According to "Apple iPad Sales Accelerate," *Wired Magazine*, June 23, 2010, http://www.wired.com/gadgetlab/2010/06/apples-ipad-sales-accelerate-three-million-sold-in-80-days/. Apple sold more than 3 million iPads in its first eighty days after release to the U.S. market.

13. For an introduction to these many different vantage points on openness, see work by Eric Raymond, Yochai Benkler, Eric von Hippel, and Harold Varmus. Raymond's classic book is *The Cathedral and the Bazaar: Musings on Linux and Open Source by an Accidental Revolutionary* (Sebastopol, Calif.: O'Reilly, 2001). Benkler's impressive and somewhat daunting book is *The Wealth of Networks* (New Haven, Conn.: Yale University Press, 2006). Von Hippel's most recent book is *Democratizing Innovation* (Cambridge, Mass.: MIT Press, 2005). Varmus's statement of why he helped to create the Public Library of Science is, with P. Brown and M. Eisen, "Why PloS Became a Publisher," *PloS Biology*, Oct. 13, 2003, e36, which can be found at the library's Web site, http://www.plosbiology.org/article/info:doi/10.1371/journal.pbio.0000036.

14. H. Chesbrough, *Open Innovation* (Boston: Harvard Business School Press, 2003), and *Open Business Models* (Boston: Harvard Business School Press, 2006).

15. This is explored at some length in *Open Innovation*, especially Chapters Two and Three, in an exposition of the closed model of innovation, in which a company tries to corner the market on useful knowledge, and the emergence of the Open Innovation model. In the latter model, it is taken as given that there is too much useful knowledge for any one firm

to control. Instead, the way forward is to adopt innovation processes that incorporate external ideas, along with internal ideas, in the R&D process.

16. There are some differences that become apparent to users when they complete a transaction on the Amazon site. Usually the Amazon Prime shipping program does not apply to third-party merchandise purchased on Amazon, and service and support queries usually have to be directed to the selling merchant.

17. Chesbrough, *Open Business Models,* p. 201.

CHAPTER 5

1. See H. Chesbrough and R. Rosenbloom, "The Role of the Business Model in Capturing Value from Innovation," *Industrial and Corporate Change,* 2002, *11*(3), 529–555, for a more academic treatment of this definition and its roots in the earlier business strategy literature. That article also points out the importance of the cognitive element of the business model, which is absent from most definitions of the topic. Most of the academic work on business models has been done in the so-called e-business category in order to understand how the World Wide Web changes the business model for established companies or enables new entry for new companies. Examples of such work can be found in R. Amit and C. Zott, "Value Creation in e-Business," *Strategic Management Journal,* 2001, *22,* 493–520; and M. Rappa, "The Utility Business Model and the Future of Computing Services," *IBM Systems Journal,* 2004, *43,* 32–42. For an academic survey of the topic, see J. Hedman and T. Kalling, "The Business Model Concept: Theoretical Underpinnings and Empirical Examples," *European Journal of Information Systems,* 2003, *12,* 49–59.

2. See C. Christensen, J. Hwang, and J. Grossman, *The Innovator's Prescription* (New York: McGraw-Hill, 2008), for a variety of such innovations that place the patient at the center of a new business model.

3. This is being phased in because the goal is to place six more paying seats on the aircraft by replacing some of the toilets on the plane. See S. Gordon, "Ryanair Confirms That It Will Bring in Charges for On-Board Toilets," *Mail Online,* Apr. 6, 2010, http://www.dailymail.co.uk/travel/article-1263905/Ryanair-toilet-charges-phased-in.html.

4. C. K. Prahalad and R. Bettis, "The Dominant Logic: A New Linkage Between Diversity and Performance," *Strategic Management Journal*, 1986, *7*, 485–501, introduced the notion of the dominant logic of a company.

5. Constructing business models in environments characterized by high complexity and ambiguity has much in common with Karl Weick's notion of sensemaking: "Sensemaking is about contextual rationality. It is built out of vague questions, muddy answers, and negotiated agreements that attempt to reduce confusion." See "The Collapse of Sensemaking in Organizations: The Mann Gulch Disaster," *Administrative Science Quarterly*, 1993, *38*, 628–652.

6. One of the best such studies is Amit and Zott, "Value Creation in e-Business." They chose the business model as the unit of analysis for their study and identified efficiency, complementarities, lock-in, and novelty as key aspects of business model innovation. These often conflict with the configurations of these assets held by more traditional firms considering experimenting with e-business.

7. Although it was not as clear in his early work, Clayton Christensen's concepts of "disruptive technology" in *The Innovator's Dilemma* (Boston: Harvard Business School Press, 1997) and especially the later notion of "disruptive innovation" in *The Innovator's Solution* (Boston: Harvard Business School Press, 2003), written with M. Raynor, call attention to similar barriers to business model experimentation. What disrupts incumbent firms in Christensen's story is not their inability to conceive of the disruptive technology. Like Amit and Zott, "Value Creation in e-Business," the root of the conflict in disruptive innovation is the conflict between the business model of the established technology and the business model for the emerging disruptive technology. Typically the gross margins for the latter are initially far below those of the established technology, the end customers may differ, and the required distribution channels may vary. As the firm allocates its capital to the highest available uses, the established technology is disproportionately favored while the disruptive technology is starved for resources. To quote Christensen quoting Andy Grove, former Intel CEO, "Disruptive technologies is a misnomer. What it is, is trivial technology that screws up your business model."

8. See "Happy Seventh Birthday, Apple Retail Stores," *MacDaily News,* May 19, 2008, http://www.macdailynews.com/index.php/weblog/ comments/17310/. The article quotes a study from Sanford C. Bernstein: "Apple's retail stores generate sales at the U.S.-leading rate of $4,032 per square foot a year (for comparison, Saks generates sales of $362 per square foot per year; Neiman Marcus, $611; Best Buy, $930; Tiffany & Co, $2,666." This comparison refers to sales during the year 2007.

9. S. Thomke's very useful book, *Experimentation Matters* (Boston: Harvard Business School Press, 2002), provides a useful summary of principles for effective experimentation. Although his concepts are focused on new product and process innovation, they apply equally to business models.

10. A second set of processes relates to what S. Sarasvathy calls *effectuation* in her book *Effectuation: Elements of Entrepreneurial Expertise* (Northampton, Mass.: Edward Elgar, 2008). The core idea here is that entrepreneurs do not predict the future, but instead take steps to bring the future into being. The future is made, rather than found, in this view.

11. See A. Davies, T. Brady, and M. Hobday, "Organizing for Solutions: Systems Seller vs. Systems Integrator," *Industrial Marketing Management,* 2007, *36,* 183–193, for more academic discussions of service organizations that are structured for a customer-facing front end and an operations efficiency–focused back end. In contrast, many product-based organizations have each product with its own customer-facing function and its own back-end operations unit.

12. As Andrew Davies, Tim Brady, and Michael Hobday's work has shown (see "Charting a Path Toward Integrated Solutions," *Sloan Management Review,* 2006, *47,* 39–48), the proportion of standardized and customized elements in a solution will vary according to the nature of the market (for example, lower-volume industrial products or high-volume consumer goods). In high-volume industries, the product is usually offered only as a standardized bundle, including a predefined set of services. In complex industrial settings, the solution offered varies considerably depending on the needs, capabilities, and sophistication of the customer organizations. Less experienced customers with limited internal systems–related capabilities often demand solutions comprising entirely standardized

offerings. More experienced or sophisticated customers, by contrast, may find that their needs are not met by a standardized solution.

13. Both IBM and Ericsson have a "strategic center" that manages the interfaces and flows of knowledge and resources between the two operational units. See Davies, Brady, and Hobday, "Charting a Path Toward Integrated Solutions."

14. H. Chesbrough, *Open Business Models* (Boston: Harvard Business School Press, 2006).

15. See T. Eisenmann, G. Parker, and M. Van Alstyne, "Strategies for Two-Sided Markets," *Harvard Business Review,* Oct. 2006, pp. 92–101, for this and other strategies to leverage two-sided markets.

16. For two excellent recent books on the topic of platforms and building the surrounding ecosystem, see A. Gawer and M. Cusumano, *Platform Leadership* (Boston: Harvard Business School Press, 2002), and M. Iansiti and R. Levien, *The Keystone Advantage* (Boston: Harvard Business School Press, 2004).

CHAPTER 6

1. "Xerox Pushes Services That Eliminate Copiers," *Wall Street Journal,* Feb. 25, 2009, p. 29.

2. Ibid.

3. "GE's Focus on Services Faces Test," *Wall Street Journal,* Mar, 3, 2009, p. B1.

4. See C. Anderson, *The Long Tail* (New York: Hyperion, 2006). Anderson points out that the long tail phenomenon is not limited to the Internet; it can apply to other businesses where the Internet is at most a minor part of the value chain.

5. This business model is not unique to GE, just as Xerox's managed print services model is not exclusive to Xerox. An interesting account of Rolls Royce's experience with a similar model can be found in "Britain's Lonely Flier," *Economist*, Jan. 10, 2009, pp. 60–62. However, both GE and Xerox have executed this model well to date.

6. These quotes are taken from an interview conducted with Ignaas Caryn, manager of business innovation and venturing at KLM, by Wim Vanhaverbeke of Hasselt University on Aug. 28, 2008, at KLM's offices in

Amsterdam. I am indebted to both men for permission to use this interview in this book.

7. See D. Fasnacht, *Open Innovation in the Financial Services* (Berlin: Springer, 2009). Fasnacht develops extensive evidence of the deep specialization of knowledge that has taken hold in financial services (despite weak formal protections for intellectual property and the corresponding business benefits of providing complete financial solutions to clients, wherever those solutions originate). These correspond well to the economies-of-scope discussion in Chapter Four of this book. Full disclosure: I wrote the Foreword to Fasnacht's book.

8. For a wonderfully written treatment of a series of organizational innovations in financial services that led to other business model innovations, see Charles Ellis's book: *The Partnership: The Making of Goldman Sachs* (New York: Penguin Press, 2008). This book covers the entirety of Goldman Sachs history up to 2008 and thus regrettably misses the troubles of more recent times. But it masterfully relates some of the key transformations that caused a very small, undercapitalized partnership to rise to the very top of the investment banking world.

A few of those transformations fit well with the story told about Merrill Lynch here. One was the use of openness in the equity block trading business. This was an area of strength for Goldman in an early period, but was now under threat from larger, more reputable, and better-financed competitors such as Salomon Brothers. Instead of simply fighting Salomon, Goldman hit on the strategy of "give-ups": sharing up to 50 percent of its commissions with partners whose investment research brought in the trading business. This made research more attractive for competitors, while discouraging firms with strong research from developing block trading expertise (since Goldman already had it and would cut them in on the commissions without the firms' having to develop their own skills, and risk their own capital). As Goldman's strength grew, it had more leverage in negotiating the levels of give-ups with those supplying research that drove deals. And it also developed a strong internal research organization over time.

Another transformation came in private placements. Goldman had a substantial private wealth management business, so some of its clients were looking for investments with particular characteristics (say, a

218

ten-year bond at such-and-such a rate of interest). It could pool those clients and approach borrowers (such as a utility company) and say, "How would you like to borrow ten million dollars at such-and-such a rate?" (pp. 168–169). This allowed Goldman to provide financing to borrowers that never even went to competitive bidding and dramatically lowered investment costs for borrowing funds (such as the preparation of a prospectus).

Another example of transformation is how Goldman promoted new business development within the company. It would identify important opportunities and celebrate any and all early wins in those new areas, even if they were very small. And Goldman hit on the organizational innovation of separating client relationships from deal execution with its Goldman's Investing Banking Services model. In this model, relationship managers developed deep knowledge of their clients' businesses, while execution specialists developed expertise in particular kinds of transactions. This internal specialization proved to be extremely valuable for Goldman, as the relationship specialists knew their clients best and the execution specialists became more adept in those specialized transactions. Knitting all this together was a partnership philosophy of compensation that promoted team incentives (versus solely individual ones) and conferred most of the gains in the partnership through long-term equity compensation versus short-term bonuses.

9. For more updated information on Merrill Lynch, see "Bank of America–Merrill Lynch: A $50 Billion Deal from Hell," *Wall Street Journal,* Jan. 22, 2009, http://www.nytimes.com/2007/10/25/business/25merrill.html; and M&A Bubble Bursts—WSJ.com.

10. See David Teece's pathbreaking article, "Profiting from Technological Innovation," *Research Policy,* 2006, *15,* 285–305. Teece explores the question of when a pioneer does and does not profit from being first to innovate, a question that remains highly relevant to this day.

11. A similar situation existed in regard to distributing stock from initial public offerings (IPO), where Merrill acted as one of the underwriters of the IPO. In such cases, Merrill took a position in the stock and supported the stock's price at the time of initial offering. It actively tried to resell its position to its clients through the Merrill broker network.

Certain IPOs of hot offerings were in high demand, and the largest and most profitable Merrill clients likely got preferential access to these shares. Offerings that were less well subscribed were sold aggressively to clients through the broker network. This prompted litigation with offerings of Webvan, RedHat, VA Linux, and other IPOs in the late 1990s.

12. This is not quite complete. Merrill continued to develop and offer its own mutual funds, and those funds could and did provide monetary incentives to Merrill advisors to sell their funds. Contests in which the top sellers qualified for bonuses and rewards were frequently held. So there remained some residual conflict of interest for the Merrill advisor, who profited from the growth in his clients' portfolios but also from successfully selling Merrill-branded funds to clients. This was part of the motivation for the Merrill merger with Black Rock in 2007, so that a new entity with a strong fund management track record (Black Rock) would be responsible for developing and managing the funds rather than Merrill itself. See K. Burke, "Got Conflicts?" *Registered Rep*, Mar. 2, 2006, http://registeredrep.com/mag/finance_conflicts/.

CHAPTER 7

1. See R. Nelson (ed.), *National Innovation Systems: A Comparative Analysis* (New York: Oxford University Press, 1993), and B-A. Lundvall (ed.), *National Systems of Innovation: Towards a Theory of Innovation and Interactive Learning* (London: Pinter, 1992), for an introduction to and thoughtful analysis of national innovation systems.

2. I was fortunate to uncover some of the history of the Olympic Circle Sailing Club on a lovely evening sail with its founder, Anthony Sandberg. I also benefited from P. Dvorak, "Board of Advisors Can Help Steer Small Firms to Right Tack," *Wall Street Journal*, Mar. 3, 2008, http://online.wsj.com/article/SB120450838510206611.html.

3. "Olympic Circle" refers to an old set of sailing markers outside the Berkeley Marina that were used for racing. Racers had to travel to each part of the circle as part of the race course. With the passage of time, the Olympic Circle has fallen into disuse. So the sailing club is now known as the OCSC, with the meaning of the initials known only to those curious enough to ask.

4. See Benjamin Gomes-Casseres, *The Alliance Revolution: The New Shape of Business Rivalry* (Cambridge, Mass.: Harvard University Press, 1996), and James Bamford, Benjamin Gomes-Casseres, and Michael Robinson, *Mastering Alliance Strategy: A Comprehensive Guide to Design, Management, and Organization* (San Francisco: Jossey-Bass, 2003).

5. See R. Normann and R. Ramirez, "From Value Chain to Value Constellation: Designing Interactive Strategy," *Harvard Business Review*, 1993, *71*(4), 65–77, and W. Vanhaverbeke and M. Cloodt, "Open Innovation in Value Constellations," in H. Chesbrough, W. Vanhaverbeke, and J. Wes (eds.), *Open Innovation: Researching a New Paradigm* (New York: Oxford University Press, 2006).

6. See H. Chesbrough, *Open Business Models* (Boston: Harvard Business School Press, 2006), for more on these innovation intermediaries.

7. I had the pleasure of having lunch with Syed Hasanain to discuss CSI at its Berkeley, California, offices, on June 4, 2010. See also N. Wilson, "Engineers Software Locally, Sells Globally," *San Francisco Business Times*, May 7, 2004, http://www.bizjournals.com/eastbay/stories/2004/05/10/smallb1.html.

8. See the company's Web site for this and other successes: http://www.csiberkeley.com/article_dom.html.

9. See A. Arora, A. Fosfuri, and A. Gambardella, *Markets for Technology: The Economics of Innovation and Corporate Strategy* (Cambridge, Mass.: MIT Press, 2001), for more on specialized engineering firms and their role in petroleum refineries.

10. See MTV's Wikipedia entry at http://en.wikipedia.org/wiki/MTV.

11. G. Slowinski and M. Segal, *The Strongest Link* (New York: Amacom, 2003). The core insight of this book is that any successful alliance involves at least three sets of interactions. The first is between the two companies. But the second is between the negotiator for company A and other managers in her company, while the third is between the negotiator for company B and other managers in his company. Understanding the internal negotiations helps to structure and manage the alliance better over time.

12. See A. Gawer and M. Cusumano, *Platform Leadership: How Intel, Microsoft, and Cisco Drive Industry Innovation* (Boston: Harvard Business School Press, 2002). Marco Iansiti and Roy Levien also explore these benefits in "Strategy as Ecology," *Harvard Business Review*, Mar. 2004, pp. 68–78.

13. See J. Hagedoorn, "Inter-Firm R&D Partnerships: An Overview of Major Trends and Patterns Since 1960," *Research Policy*, 2002, *31*, 477–492. The National Science Foundation now reports data on collaborative R&D activities between firms, finding that more than 3 percent of all private R&D spending in 2003 went to collaborative activity. The report, though, does not specify the respective sizes of the collaborating firms. Nonetheless, it is telling that NSF is now keeping statistics on such collaborations.

14. Some recent examples of these companies are documented in A. Gawer and M. A. Cusumano, *Platform Leadership: How Intel, Microsoft, and Cisco Drive Industry Innovation* (Boston: Harvard Business School Press, 2002). In addition to the companies named in the title, Palm is another such company. The book also looks at some failure cases, giving it a balanced, scholarly perspective.

15. My colleague Eric von Hippel pioneered this thinking. First, his classic book, *The Sources of Innovation* (New York: Oxford University Press, 1988), documented the important role that users play in many innovations. His more recent book, *Democratizing Innovation* (Cambridge, Mass.: MIT Press, 2005), extends his analysis to new industries like open source software and deepens the analysis of users' motives for voluntarily contributing to innovation without receiving a financial award.

    This important work has also led to some conceptual confusion. Some scholars, including von Hippel, refer to "open and distributed innovation." Alert readers will note that while there are many similarities (collaboration with users, customers, suppliers; the value of bottom-up versus top-down innovations), there are also important differences. In my earlier work, *Open Innovation* (written two years before *Democratizing Innovation*, by the way), the business model is an important element of how businesses look outside for ideas and technologies and for what ideas and technologies they let go to the outside. There is no business model anywhere in von Hippel's work. To the contrary, he focuses on the very absence of such a business model in the many innovations he studies.

Von Hippel is clearly most interested in the initial stages of innovation (the invention stage). Once the idea is prototyped and begins to spread within a user or hobbyist community, von Hippel's interest is sated. The fact that most of these go on to become profitable lines of business for profit-seeking companies is seldom noted and never analyzed. Instead, his interest is to find the next example of a user-led invention. To me, the innovation journey is not over unless and until the offering is solving customers' problems in the market. And indeed, I argue that one can be inventive without being innovative, and vice versa. We are witnessing markets between research and development where business models play a critical role.

I worry that acolytes of von Hippel's thinking may underestimate the implications of a business model for the eventual use of their contributions. Corporations have certainly taken note of user innovations and have begun to construct business models to benefit from them. One particularly thoughtful example of this comes from Scott Cook's experience at Intuit. See his "The Contribution Revolution," *Harvard Business Review*, Oct. 2008, pp. 60–69. If contributing users are not alert to this, they risk being involuntarily co-opted by a corporate agenda they may not even understand, let alone agree with. Of course, many users delight in participating in corporate-sponsored communities to improve products and services. But that is not the thrust of von Hippel's interest, which focuses on self-actualizing hobbyists.

CHAPTER 8

1. See Tom Kelley's insightful book, *The Art of Innovation* (London: Profile Business, 2002), and also his second, equally valuable book, *The Ten Faces of Innovation* (New York: Doubleday, 2005), for vivid descriptions and examples of how design firm IDEO listens to customers to uncover unexpressed needs. Jeneanne Rae at Peer Insight (www.peerinsight.com) has also shared some excellent examples of listening to what customers do, as well as what they say. She used to work at IDEO and maintains a blog at BusinessWeek.com on innovation in services.

2. See M. Roberts and W. Sahlman, "Amazon.com 2002," case 9–803–098 (Boston: Harvard Business School, 2002), for a good but somewhat dated introduction to the company. My attempts to talk directly to executives at the company were not successful, so I have had to rely on third-party and public sources for this account, a lack of openness from Amazon, which is a pity.

3. Ibid., p. 5.

CHAPTER 9

1. For a stimulating discussion of these issues, see A. Wooldridge, "The World Turned Upside Down," *Economist,* Apr. 15–21, 2010, http://www.economist.com/specialreports/displayStory.cfm?story_id=15879369&source=hptextfeature.

2. My colleague Clay Christensen is the creator of the concept of disruptive technologies. See *The Innovator's Dilemma* (Boston: Harvard Business School Press, 1997) for the foundational exposition of this concept, and *The Innovator's Solution* (Boston: Harvard Business School Press, 2003) for a useful update. Although the concept of disruptive technologies was developed in products, Christensen's own thinking has evolved to examine disruption in services too. See *The Innovator's Prescription* (New York: McGraw-Hill, 2008) and *Disrupting Class* (New York: McGraw-Hill, 2008) for applications of disruptive thinking in health care and education, respectively.

3. The facts in this section were taken from an earlier chapter I wrote, "Constructing and Managing Innovation in Business Networks," in J. Word (ed.), *Business Network Transformation* (San Francisco: Jossey-Bass, 2009).

4. See Asian Paints, "History," http://www.asianpaints.com/corporate_information/history.aspx.

5. Asian Paints, "Corporate Information," http://www.asianpaints.com/corporate_information/vision.aspx.

6. P. Khicha, "Asian Paints," *Brandchannel,* Oct. 13, 2008, http://www.brandchannel.com/features_webwatch.asp?ww_id=402.

7. Asian Paints also cleaned up its brand confusion by phasing out many of its subbrands that were detracting from the overall company image. "Asian

Paints: Every Color Tells a Story," *Marketing Practice,* Mar. 17, 2008, http://marketingpractice.blogspot.com/2007/03/asian-paints-every-color-tells-story.html.

8. Ibid.

9. Given the complexity of the Asian Paints distribution channel and the thousands of channel participants in between the company and its end customers, this was a daunting task to accomplish. This solution required a secure Web interface enabling leads from the help line to be forwarded to a Home Solutions service provider for handling. A service provider might be an independent home painting firm or interior designer, for example, in the Asian Paints network. The home solutions provider (generally the party contracting with the end customer and collecting the payment for the work) was responsible for using the system to perform all major tasks associated with a job: scheduling appointments, recording completion of site surveys, submitting job estimates, ordering paints through Asian Paints dealers, recording progress of jobs, invoicing customers, and conducting customer satisfaction surveys. Asian Paints provided these IT services to its approved Home Solutions partners at no charge.

10. "Benefits with Enterprise SOA," *SAP Global,* Nov. 29, 2007, http://www.sap.com/about/newsroom/news-releases/press.epx?pressid=8640.

11. See J. Word (ed.), *Business Network Transformation* (San Francisco: Jossey-Bass, 2009), for a discussion on the role that coordinators must play in business network transformation initiatives. In that same volume, see J. Hagel, J. Brown, and G. Kasthurirangan, "Driving Collaborative Success in Global Process Networks," which discusses Li and Fung as orchestrators who weave together the activities of numerous external parties into a coherent offering.

12. This section relies on material developed by Professors Lei Lin and Guisheng Wu, also of Tsinghua University, for a Chinese language textbook on services management: "Strategy Transition of ShaanGu Group," in *Service Management: Management of Convergence Enhancement Between Manufacturing and Service* (Beijing: Tsinghua University Press, 2007). Professor Lin was a visiting scholar at Berkeley in 2010 and introduced me to this work (in English). I am indebted to

him for translating this work. Professors Lin and Wu are pioneering scholars in the area of services innovation in China. Their work shows once more that the Chinese are not going to content themselves with success in the manufacturing sector. They see that greater prosperity for their economy lies in moving up the value chain and extending their activities into the services sector.

CHAPTER 10

1. For critiques of modern agriculture and the importance of local, organic food trends, see M. Pollan, *The Omnivore's Dilemma* (New York: Penguin Press, 2006). But note that despite such critiques, no one wants to return to the low farm productivity of a century ago.

2. See National Academy of Engineering, *The Impact of Academic Research on Industrial Performance* (Washington, D.C.: National Academies Press, 2003). This study examined the impact of academic research in five sectors of the economy. Three of these were product sectors, and the impact of academic research here was substantial. However, the other two sectors were services sectors, and here the impact was more negligible.

3. See Alan Krueger's entertaining interview with William Baumol, where this idea is discussed in more depth: A. B. Krueger and W. J. Baumol, "An Interview with William J. Baumol," *Journal of Economic Perspectives,* 2001, *15,* 211–231. The interview also covers other contributions by Baumol, a highly creative and productive economist.

4. H. Chesbrough, *Open Innovation: The New Imperative for Creating and Profiting from Technology* (Boston: Harvard Business School Press, 2003).

5. There are college courses on services management, services engineering, service operations, services marketing, and so forth. But as these titles suggest, each area treats services as a subset of a larger discipline—one that is based on the earlier delineations of agriculture or manufacturing.

6. See S. Vargo and R. Lusch, "Evolving to a New Dominant Logic for Marketing," *Journal of Marketing,* 2004, *68,* 1–17. This article takes the Prahalad and Bettis notion of dominant logic (which was developed for a firm) and applies it to an academic discipline (marketing): C. K. Prahalad and R. Bettis, "The Dominant Logic: A New Linkage Between Diversity and Performance," *Strategic Management Journal,* 1986, *7,*

485–501. Like Prahalad and Bettis, Vargo and Lusch argue that the earlier dominant logic (based on products and manufacturing) is creating an inertia that is getting in the way of a new logic based on a services economy.

7. According to Vargo and Lusch, "Evolving to a New Dominant Logic for Marketing," part of the problem is that the dominant logic of a goods-centered economy is focused on tangible resources, transactions, and production processes that embed value in artifacts that can be stored for deferred use or resale. However, an emerging services-centered dominant logic is evolving as the economy shifts increasingly to a postindustrial knowledge economy. The dominant logic of a services-centered economy is focused on intangible resources, relationships, and production processes that co-create value through performance.

8. Ian Miles of the University of Manchester disputes the idea that the academy is badly lagging behind industry with regard to services innovation (personal communication to the author, Nov. 17, 2004). However, in his recent review, "Service Innovation," in P. Maglio, C. Kieliszewski, and J. Spohrer (eds.), *Handbook of Service Science* (New York: Springer, 2010), he notes that "exploring Service Innovation, then, means grappling with the combination of two ambiguous and multifaceted concepts. The relevant bodies of research and practice are fragmented and often poorly interconnected. While there are many limitations in existing research, there have been substantial achievements—despite the double ambiguity" (p. 513). At the conclusion of his review (p. 527) he observes, "We cannot assume [services innovation] follows the patterns and is organized through the mechanisms familiar in manufacturing activities. Our approaches to innovation will have to extend beyond emphasis on artifacts and technological innovation, and pay more attention to changes in business processes and market relationships that involve service and organizational as well as technological dimensions." I am in complete agreement with his statements, suggesting that perhaps we have more that unites us than we have that divides us in the assessment of where we are as an academy with regard to services innovation.

9. R. Rust, "A Call for a Wider Range of Service Research," *Journal of Service Research*, 2004, 6, 211.

10. See J. Tidd and F. Hull, *Service Innovation: Organizational Responses to Technological Opportunities* (London: Imperial College Press, 2003). A useful overview of this balkanization was provided by I. Miles, "Innovation in Services," in J. Fagerberg, D. C. Mowery, and R. R. Nelson, *The Oxford Handbook of Innovation* (New York: Oxford University Press, 2005). Some of the best academic research on innovation in services is coming out of northern Europe and the United Kingdom. See also Miles, "Innovation in Services." B. Tether, "Do Services Innovate (Differently)? Insights from the European Innobarometer Survey," *Industry and Innovation*, 2005, *12*, 153–184.

11. See National Academies of Engineering, *The Impact of University Research on Industrial Performance*, p. 8. I also called attention to this in my article, "A Failing Grade for the Academy," *Financial Times*, Sept. 25, 2004, p. A4. A more complete discussion of the barriers to universities embracing services can be found in H. Chesbrough and J. Spohrer, "A Research Manifesto for Services Science," *ACM*, 2006, *49*, 35–40. Universities can and do change, albeit slowly. There are some signs of change already, with an annual academic research conference, Frontiers in Services, becoming popular, and *Service Research Journal*, an academic journal, recently launched. But these are only small, initial steps. Much, much more needs to be done before services research becomes a significant part of university research activity.

12. I had a personal experience on the funding difficulties in this area. I approached the National Science Foundation for funding for a conference on services innovation. After some back and forth, my proposal was rejected, with the explanation that such a conference would simply result in U.S. jobs moving to offshore locations like India. I could not have disagreed more, but no money was to be had from the foundation. I did hold the conference at Berkeley, with funding from the Finnish national technology agency, Tekes. Tekes apparently saw the value for Finland of supporting research in the United States on services innovation, something that eluded my referees at the National Science Foundation.

13. See H. Chesbrough, *Open Business Models* (Cambridge, Mass.: Harvard Business School Press, 2006), for an analysis of business models and business model innovation.

14. This case is documented in H. Chesbrough and A. Davies, "Advancing Services Innovation: Five Key Concepts," in P. Maglio, C. Kieliszewski, and J. Spohrer (eds.), *Handbook of Service Science* (New York: Springer, 2010).

15. See E. Brynjolfsson and S. Yang, "Information Technology and Productivity: A Review of Literature," *Advances in Computers*, 1996, *43*, 179–214. See also E. Brynjolfsson, "Beyond Computation: Information Technology, Organizational Transformation and Business Performance," *Journal of Economic Perspectives*, 2000, *14*, 23–48. For a more skeptical view, see R. Gordon, "Does the 'New Economy' Measure Up to the Great Inventions of the Past?" *Journal of Economic Perspectives*, 2000, *14*, 49–74.

16. E. Brynjolfsson and S. Yang, "Intangible Assets: How the Interaction of Information Systems and Organizational Structure Affects Stock Market Valuations," mimeograph, MIT and the Wharton School, 1999, p. 30.

17. Reverse innovation is discussed in J. Immelt, V. Govindarajan, and C. Trimble, "How GE Is Disrupting Itself," *Harvard Business Review*, Oct. 2009, pp. 56–65. A downloadable version of the article is available through GE at this link: http://www.gereports.com/reverse-innovation-how-ge-is-disrupting-itself/.

THE AUTHOR

Henry Chesbrough is best known as the Father of Open Innovation. He is an adjunct professor at the Haas School of Business at the University of California-Berkeley, where he heads the Center for Open Innovation. Previously he was an assistant professor of business administration, and the Class of 1961 Fellow at the Harvard Business School. He holds a Ph.D. in business administration from the University of California-Berkeley, an M.B.A. from Stanford University, and a B.A. from Yale University.

His research and writing focus on managing technology and innovation. In his first book, *Open Innovation* (Harvard Business School Press, 2003), he discussed why companies must access external as well as internal technologies and take them to market through internal and external paths. This book was named a Best Business Book by *Strategy and Business* magazine and the Best Book on Innovation on NPR's *All Things Considered*. It has been translated into eight languages. Chesbrough coedited an academic version of *Open Innovation* with Wim Vanhaverbeke and Joel West: *Open Innovation: Researching a New Paradigm* (Oxford University Press, 2006).

His third book, *Open Business Models* (Harvard Business School Press, 2006), extended his analysis of innovation to business model innovation, intellectual property management, and markets for innovation. It was named one of the ten best books on innovation in 2006 by *BusinessWeek* and is being translated into six languages.

This newest book studies open innovation in the area of services and examines the business model implications of shifting from products to services.

Chesbrough's academic work has been published in leading management and academic journals. He is a founder of Epilepsy.com and the Epilepsy Therapy Project. He is an advisor to the American Chemical Society, the Green Exchange, InnoCentive, NetBase, New Venture Partners, and Open Innovation Community Web site.

Prior to embarking on an academic career, he spent ten years in various product planning and strategic marketing positions in Silicon Valley companies. He worked for seven of those years at Quantum Corporation, a leading hard disk drive manufacturer and a Fortune 500 company. Previously he worked at Bain and Company. He can be reached at henry@openinnovationcorp.com.

INDEX

232